From Connemara to Cock o' the North

Railway Journeys in Ireland and Scotland, 1920–1950

Laurence Liddle

COLOURPOINT

Dedication

This book is dedicated to the memory of the late Robin Clements, George Mahon and Kevin Murray, whose writings have provided the author with so much of his knowledge of Irish railways.

6 5 4 3 2 1

© Colourpoint Books and Laurence Liddle
Newtownards 2002

Designed by Colourpoint Books,
Newtownards
Printed by Nicholson & Bass Ltd

ISBN 1 898392 67 6

Colourpoint Books

Unit D5, Ards Business Centre
Jubilee Road
NEWTOWNARDS
County Down
Northern Ireland
BT23 4YH
Tel: 028 9182 0505
Fax: 028 9182 1900
E-mail: info@colourpoint.co.uk
Web-site: www.colourpoint.co.uk

About the Author

Laurence Liddle, a retired chartered surveyor, was born in the north Dublin suburb and fishing village of Howth in 1915. He has no doubt that his lifelong interest in railways owes its beginnings to the fact that for the first ten years of his life he lived beside the Howth branch of the Great Northern Railway (Ireland), whose regular passenger trains provided a constant interest. Subsequent residence elsewhere in Ireland (and for a short time in Scotland) extended his railway knowledge which was again increased by regular rail travel in the 1940s, 1950s, and 1960s. He has been privileged to have travelled extensively throughout Ireland and occasionally in other countries, on steam, diesel and electric locomotives. As well as numerous articles in Irish railway publications, and very occasional contributions to the magazine *Sea Breezes*, Laurence has written *Steam Finale* (London Area of the Irish Railway Record Society, 1964) and *Passenger Ships of the Irish Sea 1919–1969* (Colourpoint Books, 1998). He is a founder member and a past chairman of the Railway Preservation Society of Ireland and has been a member of the Irish Railway Record Society for almost fifty years. Since September 1989 he has lived in Australia, but makes regular visits back to Ireland.

Cover Illustrations

The two locomotives after which this book is named – 4-4-0 No 7 *Connemara* of the MGWR, Ireland, and P2 class 2-8-2 No 2001 *Cock o' the North* of the LNER (Norman Whitla).

Contents

Acknowledgements

Many people have helped in the production of this book, and I gladly acknowledge my indebtedness to them all, and most particularly to publishers Norman and Sheila Johnston, editor Ronnie Hanna and all others at Colourpoint Books.

So far as possible, the names of photographers have been noted, and I thank them all. However, many people have helped me to locate and acquire illustrations. Sean Kennedy went to considerable trouble in supplying nearly all of the GSR/CIÉ photos, and Norman McAdams was a vital liaison man between Sean in Ireland and myself in Australia. Des Fitzgerald and Bill Scott were my sources for most of the GNR(I) illustrations whilst Nelson Poots was my e-mail linkman with Bill. William Robb's contribution of 1930s pictures was particularly welcome. Alan Brown suggested that I contact the Historical Model Railway Society for pictures of London and North Eastern locomotives, and Gerry Arundel and Tony Brown of that society provided the prints. I am also grateful to Barry Hoper of the Transport Treasury for supplying LMS and LNER photos around Edinburgh.

Finally, as always, to my wife Katharine my grateful appreciation of her encouragement and support.

Introduction

Although I can recall one or two instances of rail and sea travel dating from before 1920, it is only from the latter year onward that I have reasonably accurate railway memories. For all but six of the years between my birth in 1915 and 1989 I lived in Ireland, approximately 42 in the Dublin area and 26 in Northern Ireland, with regular comings and goings between the two. The six non-Irish years comprised four in Scotland and two in England.

During the entire period up to 1949 I travelled regularly, and from 1949 onwards frequently, to and from England, and occasionally Scotland. I also made several trips to continental Europe, particularly after 1961; but although during these latter excursions I was a keen observer of such railway scenes as came my way, my European journeys, with two exceptions, were not made for railway purposes.

I visited Australia a number of times between 1974 and 1988, and in 1989 became a permanent resident there. From the railway point of view the move had the advantage of considerably extending my knowledge, but the disadvantage was that in the process of choosing which books and papers to bring and which to dispose of before leaving Ireland, much material that would have been helpful in compiling this book was left behind. However, it is a consolation to know that anything of particular interest or value which did not come with me to Australia, is now in the Irish Railway Record Society's collection in Dublin.

What appears in the following pages is based largely on memory, without benefit of reference to notes or documents other than a GNR(I) working timetable for 1938, a 1953 public timetable from the same company, and various articles and letters which I have had published in the *Journal of the Irish Railway Record Society* and *Five Foot Three*, the magazine of the Railway Preservation Society of Ireland.

Inevitably there are errors of omission and emphasis and also, no doubt, inaccuracies, due to the influence of 87 years and more on my mental processes. I apologise for all these shortcomings, but nevertheless hope that my recollections may provide, for at least some readers, as much interest in the reading as they did for me in the compilation.

The recollections are not exhaustive; they do not deal equally with all the companies mentioned, nor indeed with all sections of any one company. During the period covered in the book I lived, at various times, in several different areas of Dublin city and suburbs, and in two areas of County Down. Hence it is the main line and the Howth and Warrenpoint branches of the Great Northern Railway (Ireland) and the south-eastern suburban section of the Great Southern Railways/Coras Iompair Éireann which provide most of my memories. I hope, however, that readers whose interests are centred on the Midland Great Western and Great Southern and Western sections of GSR/CIÉ, or on the lines of the Northern Counties Committee, may also find something engaging in what I have written. I do regret that I have only been able to produce very brief references to the Belfast and County Down Railway (BCDR), the Donegal, the Sligo Leitrim and the Dundalk, Newry and Greenore concerns. More could have been said about the Great Northern – and particularly the Portadown to Omagh section, over which I was a frequent traveller in the 1950s and early 1960s – but having written specifically about the 'Derry Road' (*Journal of the Irish Railway Record Society*, Autumn 1962) and considering the wealth of information on Irish railways recorded in print and on film over the past 40 years, I have decided to draw the line at 1950.

I am grateful to my good friend David Murray, editor of the *Journal of the Irish Railway Record Society*, for permission to reprint here some items which have appeared in that publication.

My four years in Scotland enabled me to learn a fair amount about the workings of the North British section of the LNER, and also gave me at least a superficial acquaintance with the former Caledonian and Highland lines of the LMS. Consequently I have thought it appropriate to devote a chapter to my Scottish memories.

I have been fortunate in having known many railway men of all grades, from general manager to boy porter, and mechanical engineer to cleaner, the great majority of whom have contributed in varying degrees to my railway knowledge, and several of whom became valued friends. The list of names would almost make a book in itself; two, however, call for special mention: Campbell Bailie, Operating Superintendent and later Traffic Manager of the Great Northern, and after its break up, of the Ulster Transport Authority; and the late Brian Patterson, Rail Control Officer (Personnel) and later Assistant Railways Manager of Coras Iompair Éireann. Among other things, I am indebted to each of these senior officers (and to the late Willie Marshall of the NCC/UTA) for having been

privileged to travel many hundreds of miles on steam and diesel locomotives, ranging across Ireland from Derry to Cork, Bangor to Tralee, and innumerable places in between. An account of some of my steam footplate journeys was published by the London Area of the Irish Railway Record Society, under the title *Steam Finale*, in 1964.

I have no doubt that the good relations that I enjoyed with many railway officers ultimately derived from the esteem in which my father, the late Laurence Henry Liddle FRICS, was held, in both his professional and personal capacities, by all those with whom he came into contact as Rating and Valuation Consultant to the various Irish railway undertakings. It is a particular pleasure for me to recall that as well as aiding the growth of my youthful interest in railways, he was the means of my being able as an adult to develop this interest to a greater degree than might otherwise have been possible. I still remember my father's stories about pre-1914 travel on the Midland Great Western as vividly as I recall a tale told, in the 1950s, about the high drama associated with the failure of the locomotive of a Great Northern mainline express at Goraghwood.

Laurence Liddle
Chatswood, New South Wales, 2002

A Note on Station Names

Many readers will know that the three Dublin stations of Heuston, Connolly and Pearse were known as Kingsbridge, Amiens Street and Westland Row respectively until Easter 1966, when they were renamed in memory of prominent participants in the Rising of 1916. Throughout this book I have used the old names, except in the case of references to events which occurred after April 1966, in which cases the present designations have been used.

Ireland

Showing the railway network
between the wars

Part One: The Inter-War Years

1 Early Days – The Howth Branch and the Hill Tramway

I imagine that most railway devotees have, within their general interest, a specific one related perhaps to a particular aspect of operation or development, or perhaps to a particular railway or branch.

My own special interest is the Great Northern Railway of Ireland – despite the company having suffered severe amputations as long ago as 1957 and having been done to death by politicians the following year. Even allowing for the influence of much travelling on the Great Northern, and for a short while part-time employment by the company, I have no doubt that the main factor in shaping my interest was that between the ages of five and ten and a half I lived on the Burrow Road, Sutton, on the north side of Dublin. My house faced the lines of the Howth branch and was separated from them merely by the widths of a front garden and a road. I discount the possibility that because I was born beside Howth harbour I was a GNR(I) addict from the year nought.

What was there to be seen by a very young railway enthusiast on the Howth branch in the early 1920s? To be truthful, not a great deal so far as variety was concerned. At that time the normal weekday passenger service between Dublin Amiens Street station and Howth was

at approximately hourly intervals, and although the trains did not necessarily leave Dublin exactly on the hour they were referred to locally as 'the ten', 'the eleven' and so on. The only break in the otherwise hourly sequence of invariably three-coach trains, starting with 'the seven going down' and finishing with 'the eleven going back', was that there was no train from Dublin at around midday except on Saturdays. I do not remember the details of Sunday services.

On weekdays the first down and last up trains were mixed. Occasionally, if there was some reason to get up early, I saw the former but usually I just heard it. I never saw the corresponding up evening working. Children were constrained to keep early hours in those days, no doubt assisted by the absence not only of TV, but even (in the early 1920s) of radio (the 'wireless'). My recollection of the ten-ton goods brake vans used on the mixed trains derives principally from frequent contemplation of these vehicles in the siding on the north side of the then single platformed Howth station. I rarely saw one of them in motion at the tail of a train. These brake vans contained passenger compartments labelled 'Drovers' which were used by cattle handlers accompanying their livestock. The drovers' compartments were primitive, their only source of natural light being the drop lights in the doors whilst their seats were of bare wood.

The three coaches on the regular Howth trains were always bogies. Often one would be of the former rail motor 'Lisburn' type, which, owing to their wide side windows and sometimes coupe windows in the ends, I and other small boys used to call 'observation cars'. One of us must have heard or read about US and Canadian railways at an early age. Certainly Lisburn meant nothing to six-year-old Sutton dwellers in 1921 (and doubtless vice versa). I do not think that my friends and I ever got so far as to differentiate between other types of bogie coach, though in view of the importance of season ticket holders who travelled second class, there was a greater choice of 'seasons' available for superior class than for third class commuters (not that the latter word was in use outside North America in the 1920s). In those days of more pronounced class distinction (in the social and even more in the economic sense) than there is at present, third class daily travellers were probably exclusively weekly wage earners. For these passengers the purchase of a monthly, quarterly or annual 'subscription ticket', even at a better rate of discount than what was allowed on a weekly, would not have been financially viable.

I remember only two circumstances under which I saw six-wheelers on the Howth branch in the 1920s. The first was when rakes of such vehicles, kept for excursion work, were stored on the Cosh siding at Sutton. This siding, which was lifted some years ago, ran alongside the up line to the east of the crossing gates at the west end of the Burrow Road, not far from Sutton station. These gates were a source of irritation to such local residents as possessed motor cars, in that they were kept locked against the roadway on Sundays, and on weekdays were not opened until about eight o'clock and were locked again quite early in the evening. During my time at Sutton the crossing keeper was a one-armed man who must have lived somewhere in the Howth direction as one saw him walking up and down the line to and from his work, carrying his red and green flags under his remaining arm. I never discovered how he came to lose his limb; possibly he had been involved in a work-related accident and had been given this light job subsequently.

Mention of motor cars owned by residents of the Burrow Road reminds me that in 1922 or 1923 friends of my parents who lived on the road acquired a Rover 'Pup', a small open two-seater with an 8 hp air-cooled engine. One day the lady in question, who had recently learned to drive, invited my mother for a trip. All went well until when crossing Corr Bridge (the overbridge about half a mile from Howth station) the driver lost control of her vehicle and hit the railings on the west side of the bridge fairly hard. The car was still able to bring the ladies home, but there were a few bends in the metal uprights of the bridge rails. The incident was not reported, and in due course the uprights were straightened and strengthened with metal braces. These latter remained in place for very many years, possibly indeed until the bridge was rebuilt when the Howth branch was electrified. Many years later when my father was Rating and Valuation Adviser to the Great Northern, he heard that the damage had been attributed to events connected with the Irish Civil War.

The second circumstance which produced six-wheeled coaching stock at Sutton was when the Baldoyle races were held. (Sutton station was officially Sutton and Baldoyle.) On race days trains of horse boxes, with six-wheeled passenger brake vans, came from the GSWR. These may sometimes have been stabled on the Cosh siding; but the place I remember seeing them was on the siding parallel to the Hill of Howth tramway power house and shed.

Although I have indicated that I never saw

GNR(I) Class T1 4-4-2T No 188, one of the author's 'familiar friends' in the days when his age was numbered in single figures, at Howth on an 'all stations' train to Dublin. Although this picture was taken in 1957, many years after I first knew the T1s and 'Hill Trams,' the scene, apart from the rather more modern coaches and the blue and cream livery of tram No 2, could date from the 1920s. The absence of passengers on top of the tram on a sunny afternoon (note the shadows) suggests that traffic was light.

JD Fitzgerald collection

trains of six-wheeled coaches running on the Howth branch, it is likely that specials to Sutton on race days may have been of six-wheeled stock. However, since this is a book of memories I can only say that I do not remember seeing such trains.

So much for goods brakes and passenger coaches. What sort of engines worked on the branch in the early 1920s? With two exceptions, I can remember only 4-4-2Ts, the original saturated quintet, Nos 185–89, and the first five of the superheated type, Nos 1–5. All ten of these appeared to be in regular use, and I do not recall seeing Nos 185–89 before Nos 1–5, the latter batch not appearing until 1921. However, it is quite likely that before 1921 I would have been unable to read the numbers on the engines' bunkers. So whether

Nos 185–89 ceased to be stationed in Derry, Clones and Dundalk (their original locations) before 1921, I do not know. The only evidence I have which suggests that this might have been the case is that one day during the morning break at my primary school, which was on Sutton Station Road and backed on to the railway, one of the 'big boys' (he was probably all of nine years old) remarked as an up train passed, "The old fellow, a hundred and eighty five." Be that as it may, it was certainly the case that from 1921 Glover tanks were powering the Dublin suburban trains, which of course included those on Drogheda and Malahide services as well as to and from Howth.

Not that Drogheda meant a great deal to me at the age of seven or eight; so far as I was

9

GNR(I) Class T2 4-4-2T locomotive No 62 takes the main line at Howth Junction, at the head of a down 'local.' Note the old 8 ½ compartment non-corridor third class coach at the head of the train. Note also the traditional bunker-first running out of Dublin. JD Fitzgerald

Class T2 tank engine No 3 of the Great Northern at the head of a Dublin-bound train in Howth station. This loco spent nearly all of its 42 years on Dublin suburban workings, and was well known to the author in his very early years. It was the last of its class on which he set foot, shortly before it was withdrawn in 1963. Note the sign directing passengers to the Hill of Howth tram. JD Fitzgerald

concerned the Great Northern had only two features – the Howth branch and the distant roar heard from time to time when in the back garden or on the strand immediately behind it. This roar was caused by trains crossing the Malahide viaduct on the main line.

The tank engines always ran bunker first from Dublin and chimney leading from Howth; they ran around their trains at the latter station by means of a middle road between the platform line and the siding. In view of the invariable nature of these directions of running, I have often wondered was there any reason for the practice, perhaps the sighting of a particular signal. I am more inclined to think that something of this nature may have been the case since on the one occasion on which I remember seeing a tender engine on a Howth passenger train, it was running in back gear in the down direction. As Amiens Street was a terminus, and engines on the shed there normally stood facing in the down direction, one might have expected it to have been running chimney first, towards Howth. However, of much greater interest than the direction of running of this uncommon engine was the fact that it was No 170, *Errigal*, one of the largest and newest express engines at that time It was unique in that although it had been painted black, for some years it still retained its nameplates, which I believe it carried until 1927.

Apropos of black paint, it has always interested me that George Glover, from the North Eastern Railway of England, which painted its engines green, very early in his time as Mechanical Engineer at Dundalk did away with green paint for locomotives. I have a fanciful theory that as a North Eastern man he would have had a healthy contempt for the Great Northern (England) (there was precious little love lost between Darlington and Doncaster) and would not have approved of a colour scheme that resembled very closely the Doncaster style of painting. All of which

reminds me that in a book entitled *The Railways of Great Britain*, probably given to me at Christmas 1923, there appeared this sentence: "On January 1st 1923 the Great Northern became in fact what it had long been in practice, the Southern extension of the North Eastern." So much for Stirling, Ivatt and indeed Gresley who became the GNR Chief Mechanical Engineer in 1911.

Mention of *The Railways of Great Britain* reminds me that it is only relatively recently that books specifically about Irish railway subjects have become available. There were certainly no such books in the 1920s, with the result that young Irish railway devotees of my generation, while having some practical knowledge of railway operation in our own country, in terms of general information were restricted to British, and very largely English, history and examples. We read of Ivatt, Aspinall, Robinson and Maunsell, but it was very rarely that the Irish associations of these engineers were mentioned. The only reference that I can remember comes from *The Railways of Great Britain*, which stated in the Great Northern (England) chapter that, "Mr Ivatt came from the principal Irish railway."

I remember only a very few Irish illustrations in railway books which I read in the 1920s. One, in Protheroe's *Railways of the World*, showed what was entitled "Cattle Train near Derry, Great Northern Railway of Ireland"; another in one of Cecil J Allen's earlier books showed a GNR(I) up express near Adavoyle. As I grew older and my railway knowledge broadened, from about the age of 12 onwards, it would have been nice to have known for instance that the NER and GNR railways of England, about which and about whose locomotives I had read a fair amount, had produced the then Mechanical Engineers of the two largest Irish companies – Bazin (GSR) from Doncaster and Glover (GNR(I)) from Darlington.

I recall a senior GNR(I) officer telling me

that George Glover never lost close touch with his native Tyneside, despite 20 years in charge at Dundalk. Apparently on Friday afternoons he would board the 15.15 ex-Dublin at Dundalk and travel to Belfast, and thence to Larne en route to Stranraer and Newcastle-on-Tyne. He would return from the latter city late on the Sunday night and arrive in Belfast in time to catch the 10.30 Dublin express for Dundalk. Whatever other benefits Glover may have derived from this regular returning to his roots, it certainly meant that he was able to monitor the performance of his mainline express locomotives over the hardest section of their regular route.

Returning to the Howth branch and locomotives, I can remember seeing only one tender engine other than No 170 on the branch, namely Class AL 0-6-0 No 33. During the Howth herring season this engine would occasionally come down light from Dublin and return with two or three vans, presumably loaded with herrings. The vans would have come down empty on the early morning mixed train. No 33 is the engine I associate with these fish specials, but it could be that other small 0-6-0s, whose numbers I have forgotten, or never noticed, were also used. No 33 running light, making a lot of noise and with her small wheels revolving rapidly and with a correspondingly rapid movement of the side rods, was a striking sight, and was nicknamed by our family the 'crazy engine'.

What else can I say about the Howth branch? The Hill of Howth tramway was an important auxiliary to the line, but apart from observing the trams at Sutton and Howth stations, and occasionally when I dared to take a walk in the vicinity of the shed and power house at Sutton and steal a quick glance through the doors, I did not see very much of the comings and goings on the tramway. I doubt if I travelled on it more than three or four times during all the years I lived in Sutton. I do remember once, with a friend, piling a heap of sand on each rail at the request stop at the top of Saxe Lane (between the Sutton Cross and Strand Road loops). We knew that sand was used on railways to assist adhesion, and we thought that our effort would help the next tram which halted at the stop to start again. Our sand-piling labours completed, we stood back to await the result. It was not long before a tram appeared, making for Sutton. It stopped, but imagine our surprise and feelings of being unappreciated when the driver got out, advanced on us and in a most ill-tempered voice said, "Take that sand off the rails or take a summons." So our research into the adhesive properties of sand, as applied to electric traction, never progressed to a stage when practical results could be demonstrated.

In the 1920s the Hill trams, as they were always known, had, except for Nos 9 and 10 which were special vehicles and were little used, a dual colour scheme of dark reddish brown and cream. Later they acquired a 'teak' finish similar to the colour of the GNR(I) coaches, and which Nos 9 and 10 always had. The final colour scheme for Nos 1–8 was the blue and cream of the Great Northern railcars and buses, but this did not appear until some years after I left Sutton.

As well as the ten passenger vehicles there was a works car, No 11, but I do not remember ever having seen it. Nos 1–10 were double-decked with open tops. On the upper deck there were the normal reversible slatted seats on either side of a central gangway. Inside, Nos 1–8 had longitudinal seats on each side facing inwards, whilst Nos 9 and 10 had a central longitudinal seat on which passengers sat back to back facing outwards, presumably to give excursionists a view of the scenic beauties of the Hill of Howth. My recollection is that the inside seats on all cars were devoid of upholstery, and that passengers sat directly on the highly varnished slatted wooden seats, but there may have been some partial seat coverings. Certainly the seats in the downstairs part of the cars were not as well covered as those on the Dublin United Tramway Company's vehicles, which competed with the trains for the Dublin–Sutton–Howth passenger traffic.

Since this chapter deals with memories of my very early years, it is not the appropriate place to discuss the mechanical features of the cars – in the 1920s I did not have any understanding of electricity. Anyone who is interested and who can obtain a copy of the *Irish Railway Record Society Journal* No 36 (February 1965) will find much technical information in a most interesting article on the Tramway by Mr RC Flewitt. However, I do remember a couple of minor points in which the Hill trams differed from those of the DUT Co, with whose line the GNR(I) track made a 'square crossing' at Sutton Cross. The Hill trams had electric bells for communication between conductor and driver, whereas the DUT cars had gongs actuated by a rod moved by a strap on the conductor's platform. Another difference concerned the bogies: in the Great Northern type the larger (driving) wheels were at the outer ends and the carriers towards the centres of the cars; on the DUT cars these wheel positions were reversed. Yet another difference was that whilst the platforms of the Dublin cars were completely glass enclosed, the railway company's vehicles had an open space behind the stairs, over which a canvas screen could be drawn in wet weather. None of these three points of difference was important and none may be thought particularly interesting, but I mention them as an indication of the sort of feature which attracted the notice of an enthusiastic, but not very well informed, beholder in the days when his age could be measured in single figures.

The Hill tramway was single tracked with crossing loops at frequent intervals, and a further point of interest for the young traveller (or more often lineside watcher) was the signalling system. This consisted of colour lights at the loops operated by the drivers as their cars passed through.

The tramway timetable was based on connections with the trains at Sutton and Howth stations, and not on the provision of a straight through service from Sutton to Howth or vice versa. The usual service ran as follows. Soon after the arrival of a down train at Sutton, a tram, we will call it car A, left for the Hill of Howth ('the summit'). This tram, on its way towards the Hill, would cross car B coming down to give a connection into the just-mentioned train on its return journey to the city. Meanwhile a third car, C, would have left the summit for Howth station at which point it would provide connections both out of and into the train. When this latter car had returned to the summit it would find there car A already arrived from Sutton. Both vehicles would then wait until it was time for car C to proceed to Sutton and car A to continue on to Howth, to give the necessary connections for the next train. As soon as this second train had arrived at Sutton from Dublin, car B would set out again for the Hill. It will be seen therefore that a minimum of three cars 'in steam' was needed to operate the basic service.

However, I have a recollection, though I cannot be certain, that at the slackest periods of the day only two cars would be operating. This would mean that although the service between the summit and Howth was unaffected, passengers from or to the Hill via Sutton, and those using intermediate stops on the Sutton side of the Hill, would be subjected to waits at Sutton station in either direction. The tram from the summit would arrive at Sutton after the down train had arrived, but before this train arrived back on its up journey.

Leaving aside Nos 9 and 10, which were used only at times of the very highest traffic, there were up to seven cars available for the normal passenger service, so that at times such as fine summer Sundays and Bank holidays it was not difficult to have cars available to duplicate services. The reason that it was seven, rather than eight, cars that were available was because one of Nos 1–8 was used for overhead wire maintenance as a tower wagon, with scaffolding erected on its top deck – from time to time one or more would be withdrawn for regular maintenance or emergency repairs. General maintenance and running repairs were carried out in the shed at Sutton, but on occasions the cars were hauled to Dundalk works after their top hamper (the wire grill around the top) and the trolley had been removed. Regrettably, I never saw this operation.

In September 1925 I said a temporary goodbye to the Howth branch, as our family moved across Dublin to Shankill. There the GSR (former Dublin and South Eastern) station was some ten miles from the Harcourt Street terminus of the erstwhile Dublin, Wicklow and Wexford Railway (which, I think in 1907, changed its name to Dublin and South Eastern). However, just a few weeks before we moved I had my first footplate trips, on tank engine No 5, running around its train at Howth. The driver was unknown to me, but he had the right attitude towards small boys, for I had no fewer than three trips in a single week, twice in company with two friends and once by myself. On the last occasion the enginemen were accompanied by the driver's son, who did not seem to be much older than my own ten and a half years, but who had obviously already mastered the rudiments of driving. He operated regulator and reverser as if 'to the manner born,' which in a sense he had been.

2 Introduction to the Great Southern – Bray and Mullingar

Bray

I reacted to the move to Shankill with mixed feelings; it was interesting to go to a new house, but boarding school in Bray, though only two miles distant from home, was not wholly welcomed. However, I soon found new railway interests. We were not allowed off the school premises on our own, but the sights and sounds of railway operation were constant accompaniments to our lives both day and night. I must have heard Nos 461 and 462, 2-6-0s, starting the nightly Wexford goods from Bray many times before I set eyes on either. Did I ever see No 461 as DSER No 15, and with DSER lettering on the tender? The picture is certainly in my mind, but I associate it with the engine being in one of the carriage sidings to the south of the station, on the west side of the single line to Wexford. Normally one might have expected the loco to have been at Dublin's Canal Street shed on those days when she was not at Wexford. Did she perhaps, in an emergency, work a Bray local in place of its regular engine?

Aside from No 15 or 461, there were plenty of other engines to be seen during daylight hours, particularly from the school's playing field or when bathing at Bray Head during the summer. The later 1920s marked a most interesting, though by no means painless, period in the operation of the suburban services of the former 'Dirty, Slow and Easy' railway. One saw both varieties of that company's 4-4-2Ts, and also the 2-4-2Ts, but there were, in addition, strangers abroad. J15 0-6-0s, ex-GSWR 0-4-4WTs, MGWR standard

Bray in 1931 showing the new down platform. When the author first knew it, Bray had only one platform. The DSER seemed to have a particular liking for single platforms at important stations; other examples were Harcourt Street (Dublin), Dun Laoghaire and Wexford   Real Photographs 7043, courtesy CP Friel

From the 1925 amalgamation until the final puff of steam on GSR/CIÉ in 1963, almost all engines were painted a dull greyish black, without lining or ornament of any kind. Only the three 800 class 4-6-0s of 1939–40 and a few locos painted green in the 1950s, were allowed to display any colour. It is pleasant therefore to be able to see DSER 4-4-2T No 20, later GSR/CIÉ Class C2 No 455, looking resplendent in her DSER livery in 1913, two years after she had emerged from Grand Canal Street Works. She was the last locomotive to be built there. DSER photo, courtesy J Kennedy

goods and 2-4-0s, each of the two last mentioned types with their original fly away cabs, all made their contributions to motive power on both the coastal and Harcourt Street lines.

Of the former Midland engines, I can still remember *Luna*, a 0-6-0, and *Aurora*, a 2-4-0, hauling their unsymmetrical-looking trains southwards from Bray, blasting their way up the bank and round the curve at the beginning of their journeys to Greystones. I saw another sort of Midland loco at Bray station during the Christmas holidays of 1925 – *Robin*, one of the diminutive 0-6-0 tanks built for minor branch line work on their parent system, but which after the amalgamation spread all over the Great Southern, including eventually the Waterford and Tramore section. The fact that I clearly remember the name *Robin* indicates

that in December 1925 the little engine was still in MGWR livery – but what was she doing in Bray? Successful as the class was on the duties for which it was designed, and on others which could never have been imagined at Broadstone at the time of building, it would scarcely have been expected to cope with smartly timed suburban trains on Dundrum and Killiney banks. Did Bray have a regular shunting engine in 1925, or was *Robin* there on a special working?

Despite the interest of seeing unfamiliar, and sometimes to my mind strange looking engines on the local trains, there is no doubt that the chief gain for my railway interest from our move of house was that I now saw mainline Irish passenger and goods services for the first time. As far as the former was concerned, what was on offer in the down

GSR Class J19 (MGWR Class 'L') 0-6-0 No 585 heading an up suburban train at Bray in 1952. This loco has acquired an 'Inchicore' cab and chimney, but not the 'X' boiler with which many of her sisters were fitted in Great Southern days. 'Midland' engines of several types worked between Dublin, Bray and Greystones from soon after the 1925 amalgamation until almost the end of steam   *J Kennedy*

direction was nothing very spectacular – just the second Dublin–Wexford train which left Harcourt Street at about 10.30. This train was certainly a mainline one, but it was neither long nor fast; the usual make-up in the later 1920s was an ex-DSER 4-4-0 (I remember No 57, *Rathnew*, in original livery) hauling two corridor bogies, a six-wheeled brake and two or three smaller fitted vehicles. The 10.30 stopped at all 17 stations between Bray and Wexford taking, so far as I remember, something over three hours for the journey. (I could repeat all the stations by heart from my perusals of the 'Red Guide', despite its abominable print, long before I ever travelled south of Bray.)

On the whole, the 10.30 might be judged not much of a train, but it must have made quite an impression on me because it was one which I often simulated after my 'O' gauge layout had progressed beyond the stage of

0-4-0 engines and four-wheeled carriages. Once I had acquired three Bassett-Lowke coaches (two in GWR and one in LNWR colours) and a German clockwork 4-4-0, in outline resembling an LNWR 'George the Fifth' (but painted in Great Western style), this engine, two of the bogie coaches and an assortment of Hornby four-wheelers on the tail gave quite a realistic impression of the 10.30 down Wexford (apart from the colour scheme). My father gave me a great boost one day when, after I had drawn his attention to my DSER mainline 'express', he said, "Yes, I can see all the passengers and even the smuts on some of their faces." It is possible that my father had associated smuts on passengers' faces with the Dublin and South Eastern due to something he had been told by a very old man he had known about 1912 or 1913. According to this gentleman, in the earlier days of the railway between Dublin and Dun Laoghaire

(Kingstown in those days) a common practice after arriving at the latter station from the city was to go to a chemist and ask him to take the smuts out of one's eyes.

Regardless of smuts, real or imagined, in 1926 the South Eastern, the 'Cinderella' section of the Great Southern, had two trains larger and more impressive than the 10.30 down Wexford, namely the Mail and the Rosslare. I do not think that I ever saw the down Mail, as it left Bray too early in the morning to be seen from school, though like the night goods it was often heard. It was also the only one of the three daily Dublin–Wexford passenger services which operated to and from Westland Row (Pearse) station and so was not visible from Shankill. However, the up working, which was due to arrive in Bray around 19.00, was often seen from school during the summer and at Bray station during the holidays. The Mail was an altogether more substantial train than the 10.30, as regards both engine power and coaches. The former was normally provided by an ex-GSWR large 4-4-0 of the 333 (D3) or 301 (D11) classes, at that time with round-topped fireboxes. The large boilers in front of their skimpy 'Inchicore' cabs enhanced their massive appearance. On the up Mails these big engines came off at Bray and one of the suburban locos took the train on to Dublin. I use the term 'big engines' in the absolute sense – of contemporary Irish locomotives the 333s and 301s were definitely to be counted among the large ones; larger for instance, though lighter, than the Great Northern S and rebuilt Q classes.

There was a third type of 'Inchicore' 4-4-0 which I saw at Bray during the 1925–28 period – the small D14 or 60 class, at that time unsuperheated and with round-topped fireboxes. One of these often brought in the early morning Wicklow–Dublin passenger train, which gave an earlier service from Wicklow than was provided by the up morning Rosslare, and also enabled the latter to omit

stops at Newcastle and Kilcoole. The Rosslare, which commenced running from that port in 1926 (previously it had started from Wexford) was not a train which I saw often, though I once observed it arriving at Bray in the down direction behind a J15 0-6-0 whose smokebox door (quite possibly doors at that time) was (or were) red hot at the bottom. This occurrence was in winter time; the locomotive must have made quite a spectacle running down Carrickmines bank and across the high Cherrywood viaduct in the darkness.

As regards goods trains, the only ones that I saw at all frequently were the up day trains from Enniscorthy to Dublin. My chief recollection of them is that they were usually hauled by ex-DSER 0-6-0s which, with their square side-windowed cabs, I thought extremely ugly machines. It was some years before I became aware of how highly regarded these relatively small locomotives were by the men who worked them. This all goes to show that one must not be misled by appearances, a maxim which I was to remember many years later when as a commuter between Bangor and Belfast I made my first acquaintance with the big 4-6-4Ts. This time, however, the maxim operated in reverse to what had been the case with the DSER locos.

Most of my observations of South Eastern section engines were made at Bray, our house at Shankill being some distance from the station (on the Harcourt Street line). After 1927, when regular Dublin–Bray bus services started to operate, the latter were much more convenient than the railway for travelling to either Bray or the city. From what I remember of the Harcourt Street line, the passenger motive power from 1925 to 1933 was mainly provided by ex-DSER 2-4-2Ts. When I first got to know these engines I regarded them as very 'small beer'; certainly they were not to be spoken of in the same breath as the GNR(I) 4-4-2Ts. Before long, however, and despite the fact that my journeys behind them were

Great Southern and Western Railway 60 class (later GSR/CIÉ D14 class) 4-4-0 No 87 in original condition, including double smokebox doors, at Inchicore in the early 1900s. These locos, which were the principal express engines of the GSWR in the later 1890s, had a deserved reputation for fast running, which even in their later years was manifested when working the newspaper trains and piloting heavy expresses. Compare this photo with that of sister engine No 95 after rebuilding and superheating in the 1920s (page 101). Most of the class were rebuilt, Nos 62, 88 and 89 also receiving new 321 style cabs, making them, in my opinion, very handsome machines. No 61, at the time employed on suburban workings, was for a while painted green after World War Two. H Fayle, courtesy J Kennedy

relatively infrequent, I realised that they were sturdy and dependable little machines which coped well with the heavy banks on either side of Foxrock.

I have mentioned the main engine types which I remember from the late 1920s and early 1930s, but what about South Eastern carriages during the same period?

The first thing that struck me, having been used to the all-bogie make-up of the regular Howth trains, was the abundance of six-wheelers. These came from three sources. There were the native DSER vehicles with their slightly rounded cross-sections, spoked wheels and brown velvet upholstery in the first class compartments; and there were GSWR vehicles, about which all I remember is that they were from the Southern; but above all, and most prominent in my memory, were the six-wheelers from the Midland Great Western.

Most of the Midland six-wheelers were rather low, with prominent 'chimneys' for insertion of oil lamps, small windows with rounded corners, and very distinctive door furniture. This latter feature comprised the actual door handles, which were loop shaped rather than of the conventional 'T' pattern; and the grab handles which, instead of being of plain vertical design, had two right-angled bends. I do not think that any oil lamps survived until 1925 – indeed one of my most enduring early memories of Bray is of the strong smell of gas from the tank wagons which stood in a siding to the south of the passenger station and which journeyed to Inchicore for replenishment. The 'gas tanks' trains survived until well after the World War Two, and will be referred to again.

While I was writing the first draft of this reference to six-wheeled coaches, it occurred to me that probably only a small proportion of

From the late 1920s to the early 1950s the Class F2 2-4-2Ts of GSR/CIÉ were the 'maids of all work' on the south-eastern suburban services, as they had been under their original owners the Dublin and South Eastern, from as far back as the 1890s. Apart from having been provided with boilers having round-topped fireboxes, they were little changed in appearance during their long lives. However, the dull grey black paint with which they were daubed at Inchicore was a far cry from their original livery, as seen here on St Aiden. GSR/CIÉ No 433 of this class worked from 1886 to 1957, 71 years of hard, unglamorous service to the computers of south Dublin and north Wicklow; at least she got a green coat for her last few years!

H Fayle, courtesy IRRS

readers will have known what it was like to travel in one of these vehicles and that therefore a description of such travel might be interesting. I do not think that I can do better than quote what Hamilton Ellis had to say on the subject, in his book *The North British Railway*:

> The North British seemed to have quite as faithful an affection as the Great Northern for the six-wheeler on express trains. Up and down the East Coast Route they trundled, and over the length and breadth of Scotland, and in much later years they seemed, to the fanciful, to emphasise their mysterious antiquity by an everlasting reiteration of 'Zimbabwe, Zimbabwe, Zimbabwe.'

In 1959, when Ellis's book was published, Zimbabwe had not yet become the title of a country, and was known merely as the name of a mysterious group of ruins in southern Africa. To achieve an accurate rendering of the sound of the MGWR six-wheelers 'trundling' their way over the DSER suburban lines the trisyllabic Zimbabwe should be expressed in a long-drawn-out fashion, and with the emphasis on the final syllable: 'Zim-bab-we, Zim-bab-we, Zim-bab-we.'

The DSER had a few excellent and up to date non-corridor bogie carriages, and these, together with some shorter and older ex-GSWR vehicles of the same type, appeared along with the six-wheelers in the suburban trains. Another variety of suburban coach which I remember from the early days were the DSER bogies adapted for use in off-peak trains on the coastal route. These had been ordinary compartment vehicles, but the compartments were removed and the side doors permanently closed up. A single set of double doors was fitted centrally on each side, with guard's brake controls in the space between them – hence the coaches could be used singly or in pairs during the slack traffic periods.

So much for the suburban vehicles. What of those on the main line? These latter carriages were certainly corridor bogies, but what proportion were ex-DSER, and what proportion came from the Southern and the Midland, I can no longer remember. I do recall, however, travelling in an ex-MGWR bogie third in the 10.30 down Wexford train in 1930, and this vehicle will be referred to in greater detail later. I have already mentioned the make-up of the 10.30. The constituent vehicles of the Mail were more interesting in that they included a TPO (albeit a six-wheeler) and an unusual sort of dining car (ex-GSWR No 343), which as well as providing 15 seats for meal service accommodated six first class passengers in a side corridor compartment. Although the TPO worked to and from Wexford, the 'Diner' served Waterford via Macmine and New Ross, an interesting survival from the days of competition between the South Eastern and the Southern (GSWR) for the Dublin–Waterford traffic. The Mail usually consisted of four bogies, plus TPO, plus the inevitable six-wheeled brake.

For the up morning and down evening Rosslare trains I have a figure of six bogies in my mind, and I very distinctly remember travelling in the down train from Harcourt St to Bray on a winter evening when the make-up included an ex-GSWR centre-kitchen diner.

Before leaving the South Eastern, here are a few notes on stations other than Bray.

I have already mentioned Foxrock. This was an important station, with three platforms and ample carriage sidings to cope with the heavy traffic offered when the Leopardstown races were held on the course adjoining the station. As well as being a stopping place for all Dublin–Bray–Greystones suburban trains by the inland route, Foxrock and Leopardstown, to give the station its full title, was served during rush hours by additional stopping trains to and from Harcourt Street. (The name Leopardstown is not of zoological origin but refers to a medieval leper settlement.)

Percy French is credited with the immortal remark, "There are two sides to everything except Harcourt Street station," and for a city terminus handling both suburban and mainline trains Harcourt Street was an awkward and strange looking place. The station's exterior, facing on to Harcourt Street, was (and is) impressive in a modest way, and promised more than the single platform on to which one arrived after mounting a substantial number of steps. But there was a compensation which for a juvenile enthusiast more than balanced the paucity of platforms. Where else could there be found within the actual precincts of a passenger station a turntable? Moreover, this particular turntable was one on to which all incoming locos had to proceed after being hooked off, and from which, after turning, they moved to the run around loop which passed outside the further wall of the overall roofed station. Before the amalgamation, the DSER's Dublin goods yard had been at Harcourt Street, but very early in Great Southern days trains were diverted to the North Wall, which entailed their using the coastal route between Dublin and Bray. I never saw Harcourt Street goods yard in use.

Harcourt Street, with its one platform, was far from being unique on the South Eastern. Dun Laoghaire, Bray and Wexford also had single platforms. Both Bray, which got a second platform in the 1930s, and Dun Laoghaire, which had to wait until after World War Two, were places where the normal problems of operation were greatly increased by awkward layouts. The state of affairs was worse at Bray than at Dun Laoghaire for three reasons: first, because crossing gates at the north end of the station interfered with the comings and goings of trains (this was particularly restrictive from 1927 onwards when three bus companies started to operate regular Dublin–Bray services over the crossing); second, because the locomotive shed, at the east side of the running line immediately to the south of the station, was on the opposite side of the lines to the turntable, which was situated where the Greystones shuttle bay later was; and third, because the single line to Greystones and beyond could give rise to delays.

It should also not be forgotten that Bray had passenger trains to and from Dublin by both the Harcourt Street and the Westland Row routes, with the extension of some services to and from Greystones (and one each way to Wicklow), and also mainline passenger trains

and the Wexford and the Enniscorthy goods, so there was rarely a time when something was not moving at the station. All of the above was of great interest to myself in my tender years (no pun intended, and in any case most of the locos seen were tanks), but there was a snag: the platform was separated from the entrance concourse by a substantial wrought iron railing, to negotiate which one was required to be in possession of a ticket. So, usually having come from Shankill by bus, I made the best of a bad job and stood at the crossing gates.

I was not often in Dun Laoghaire station in the 1920s apart from passing through it to and from the Carlisle (mail boat) pier on our annual summer visit from Sutton to grandparents in the south of England, and hence I remember little about operations at that one-platform station. However, although undoubtedly awkward, Dun Laoghaire had

This 1928 picture of Carlisle Pier at Dun Laoghaire (the 'Mail Boat' pier), shows the awkward single-line approach from the former Dublin and South Eastern Railway's coastal suburban line. The picture also gives a good representation of the different types of passenger coach in use on short-distance services of the Great Southern Railways at the time. Many of these old vehicles lasted until the end of steam. Note the turntable. The vessel on the left has worked the afternoon service from Holyhead; her sister on the other side of the pier will take the night sailing to the Welsh port. A few non-rail passengers are on their way to embark.

J Kennedy collection

The Great Southern Railways, like the Northern Counties Committee, had no misgivings about pairing modern engines with ancient tenders. In this picture, taken at Dun Laoghaire in 1949, GSR Class J15B 0-6-0 No 717, built in 1934, is followed by an 1850 gallon tender dating from the nineteenth century. The Dublin–Bray train is typical of its period, and indeed could have been seen on the south-eastern suburban line at any time between 1925 and the end of steam. The second vehicle from the engine is of Dublin and South Eastern origin; the other coaches hail from the Great Southern and Western. J Kennedy

none of the special disadvantages of Bray. Provided that the working timetable could be drawn up so that no trains were expected to cross each other in Dun Laoghaire (in practice not between Salthill and Sandycove, the stations to the north and south respectively), matters could be coped with reasonably well, if trains ran to time. However, as well as the Dublin–Bray locals, the Wexford Mails and the goods, there were the pier trains and the inner suburban locals to and from Dalkey, and at peak periods to and from Dun Laoghaire itself. All of which ensured that business on the single through line was usually pretty brisk.

Mention of Dun Laoghaire and Dalkey reminds me that I have not yet referred to the ex-DSER 2-4-0Ts. In the mid-1920s I knew that these machines existed, but so far as I remember I never saw one of them in either Shankill or Bray. Another loco which did not

come my way for several years was the big 2-6-2T, No 850. Although it entered service in 1928 I did not see it until 1930, presumably because I left my Bray school in the former year.

The only other station in the Dublin suburban area of the GSR which I remember at all clearly from this period is Westland Row (Pearse), and for two reasons. First, I can recall travelling in a horse cab from there to Amiens Street on the way back from one of the aforementioned visits to England. The point about this recollection is that the vehicle exit from the station was down what is now one of the pedestrian exits from the north-going through platform (No 3). Second, in I think 1927, on what may have been my first visit to Dublin unescorted by an adult, I saw one of the steam railcars. I have a mental picture of flame issuing from the top of the chimney, on the face of it an unlikely happening, but scarcely a situation I would have invented. Were these cars prone to such behaviour, or perhaps difficult to fire?

Mullingar

Next to the Great Northern, the Irish railway which has always interested me most has been the Midland Great Western, and I have no doubt that this interest owes its origins to two periods of six consecutive days which I spent in Mullingar in 1926 and 1927. In August of each of these years I accompanied my father when his professional work took him to Mullingar. Between about 10.00 am and 4.00 pm we would be out in the country, but the remainder of the day, except for a short meal break, I spent at the station where there was much of interest to see, as regards both locomotives and complete trains. In 1926 there was still a fair amount of MGWR lettering on tenders and some of the engines still had their nameplates. In these years (1926–27) I saw seven different types of engine at Mullingar, five of which were 'pure' Midland Great Western.

As regards 4-4-0s, there were the large Cusack engines, as rebuilt with superheaters, and the slightly smaller and later 4-4-0s, also designed by Cusack. So far as I, in my 11 or 12-year-old ignorance was concerned, however, the only subdivision of these 4-4-0s was that between those with the rounded, slightly GNR(I) pattern of cab (as a result of rebuilding) and those whose cabs were of more conventional design. Had I known it, the former had another similarity to the Great Northern locos in that their screw reverser operated as on the S class, ie the handle was wound 'backwards' to put the engine into forward gear. These were known on the Midland as the 'crossed rod' engines, though it was well beyond the 1920s before I came across the term.

Then there were the Atock 2-4-0s, all of which during my two visits to Mullingar had their original 'flyaway' cabs. Of the six coupled

engines seen, there were the 'mixed traffics', the large wheeled 0-6-0s of Class 'F' which had been built at Broadstone and Newcastle-on-Tyne as recently as 1924, and Atock's 'standard goods', also with his unique design of cab. The 'mixed traffics' had the same semi-GNR(I) type of cab, similar to that of the 'crossed rods'. I do not remember seeing any other types of Midland Great Western locos at Mullingar, such as the heavy goods, the 'Avonsides', the 'Achill bogies' or either variety of 0-6-0T.

Of the Midland engines which I did see, the 4-4-0s were on the Dublin–Galway passenger trains and also worked on the Mullingar–Sligo branch. The 2-4-0s monopolised the Dublin–Cavan passenger trains. As well as providing a service between Dublin and Cavan, which competed with and was shorter than the Great Northern facility between the same two points, these trains also served as all-stations locals between Dublin and Mullingar. I saw the 'mixed traffics' on stock specials and also on the up Mayo line Friday relief to the Mail.

My clearest recollection of an Atock 'standard goods' at Mullingar is of No 87 (MGWR number), complete with nameplate *Bear* on the side of the boiler, on station pilot duties. Another named engine was the Cusack 4-4-0, No 7 *Connemara*, which I remember seeing at the head of the 14.45 down mainline passenger train, due into Mullingar at about 16.00. Though in post-war black livery, *Connemara* was still painted in full MGWR style. In line with the best Midland tradition, the vehicle immediately behind the tender was a six-wheeler.

But impressive as the large 4-4-0s and the 'mixed traffics' were – and the latter with their high-pitched boilers seemed most imposing to an 11-year-old who could scarcely have been expected to appreciate the limitations of their small fireboxes – there is no doubt that at that age, and with little railway experience beyond the Howth branch and Bray station, I awarded

Great Southern Railways Class D5 (MGWR Class 'A') No 545 arriving at Sligo in 1938. This locomotive was built in 1902 but was subsequently substantially rebuilt and superheated, in the process acquiring an extended smokebox, but not the improved style of cab fitted to her sisters. The train is a mixture of ex-MGWR, ex-GSW and new Great Southern vehicles. The coach immediately behind the engine is a former Midland Great Western composite. RN Clements/J Kennedy

Great Southern Railways Class D6 4-4-0 No 542 at Broadstone in the 1930s. Note the short firebox (grate area only 17.3 square feet) and the peculiarly Midland Great Western feature of the extended smokebox. This engine was one of the Midland 'C' or 'Connemara' class. The class was rebuilt, superheated and reclassified Cs in the early 1920s, some engines receiving piston valves in the process. Under the Great Southern, the erstwhile 'Connemaras' became either D6s with slide valves or D7s with piston valves. RN Clements/J Kennedy

This is absolutely vintage MGWR. Even though the photo of Atock 2-4-0 No 32 Aerial, pictured at the Broadstone, dates from many years before your 11-year-old author first made acquaintance with Mullingar in 1926, this picture could have been taken there in that year. The Cavan trains referred to in the text looked just like this one. Only the communication cord looped across the tender had disappeared by the 1920s.

H Fayle, courtesy IRRS

Ex-MGWR 'standard goods' GSR No 587 (Class J18) at Mullingar in 1939. Although these locos, and the very similar J19s, were in many ways comparable to the ex-GSWR 0-6-0s of Class J15, their firegrate area of only 16 square feet was somewhat meagre when contrasted to the 18.75 square feet of the J15s. Each type had 18" x 24" cylinders. Note the long buffers, an MGWR peculiarity.

CP Friel collection

first prize to the 'Woolwichs', which shared the Galway trains with the 4-4-0s. What a pity, I thought, that they were painted in such a dull manner (GSR all-over greyish black). Like many another embryo railway enthusiast, I was fascinated by my first close up view of the outside Walschaert's valve gear, previously only glimpsed at a distance on a few English railway journeys. My railway reading had tended to emphasise the 'neat outline' of traditional British locomotives, and to suggest none too subtly that American and continental types, with half of their innards stuck on the outside, were aesthetically beyond the pale. I did not agree – for me a 'Woolwich' starting the up Mail out of Mullingar, with moving valve gear fully visible and both the exhaust and open cylinder cocks contributing to the overall noise and impression of power, was a paragon among engines. I would not go so far as to say that there and then I lost my heart to the Midland, and foreswore my allegiance to the Great

Northern, but it was a near thing. One of the last times I was in Mullingar station was in the cab of a '121' class GM 'Bo-Bo', one of a pair heading the second weekday up Sligo passenger. As we lay stopped on the up branch track, directly opposite the tall cabin at the apex of the V formed by the up Galway and down Sligo platforms, my mind went back 62 years – I became again, for a moment, the 11-year-old standing at the platform edge and gazing, fascinated, at the 'Woolwich' and all its works.

I have earlier stated that I saw two types of non-native locomotive at Mullingar – the first was the 'Woolwich', but what about the second? Younger readers may be surprised to learn that this was the GSWR 0-4-4WT, first built in 1879 (though an earlier class was built in 1870–75). I had previously seen examples of this class on suburban work in Bray, but now I was able to make a closer acquaintance with this archaic-looking type of engine. An 0-4-4T operated the Banagher branch train which

An up Galway and Mayo Day Mail arriving at Amiens Street (now Connolly) Junction in 1951. The locomotive is Class K1a 'Woolwich' 2-6-0 No 396. By this time the Mail no longer conveyed a Sligo portion, which was run separately. Note the former MGWR bogie coach, (third from the engine), and by contrast the two modern steel-panelled vehicles at the back of the train. Apart from these latter two coaches, the whole train, from engine to tail lamp, is virtually unchanged from a 1930s makeup
                                                                                            J Kennedy

The date is 1951 and the location is the 'Gullet' between Kingsbridge (now Heuston) station and Inchicore. A heavy goods train, with a 'Woolwich' 2-6-0 at its head, would not have been a strange sight for the author during his juvenile platform saunterings at Mullingar 25 years earlier, although the Volkswagen 'beetles' would not have been in evidence. Note the full head of steam and the sanding gear in operation.

D Murray, courtesy J Kennedy

since the amalgamation had worked through to Mullingar, rather than running between Banagher and Clara only, as in GSW days. By this means, one engine could operate the services on both the Banagher and the MGWR Streamstown–Clara branches. In reference to the latter branch, one day in 1926 or 1927 when I was out in the country with my father he had occasion to call officially at Horseleap station, the only stopping place between the two ends of the branch. After he had finished his business with the station master, and had come back to the car, my father told me that the latter functionary had vouchsafed the information that in former days Horseleap had had a "grand traffic in remains", but that this (or these?) now almost all went by road. It is a pity that the Clara branch is long since gone and that road traffic has triumphed. I can conceive of many a worse final journey than from Streamstown to Horseleap, and of many a worse resting place than one within sound of that placid Westmeath–Offaly branch line.

I have said that I saw both locomotives and complete trains at Mullingar. I do not remember very much in the way of goods workings, apart from cattle trains (the sight of a beast down on the floor of a wagon, covered in excrement and scarcely able to move, has remained with me as one of the less attractive aspects of railway operation), but there was plenty of passenger traffic. Here I should mention that, in contrast to the practice which has obtained for many years of there being separate Galway, Mayo and Sligo trains from Dublin, in 1926–27 these were combined and there was only one through working per day between Broadstone and the Mayo branch (Achill and Ballina).

There were three mainline trains in each direction on weekdays: the Mail, which left Broadstone at around 07.00 or 07.30; the 14.45, which conveyed the Achill and Ballina through coaches; and the night Mail. Coming up, the early morning service and the night Mail had Galway and Sligo portions (as did the down day and night Mails) whilst the up day Mail had through vehicles from all three lines.

The down and up Mails had a dining car which ran to and from Galway. There was a second catering service, provided by a Pullman, which (in 1927) operated between Dublin and Sligo on the up morning train and on the 14.45 down. This car was one of a small number which commenced working on the GSR in 1926 (the other routes were between Dublin and Cork and Dublin and Limerick). The cars were all third class, and were similar, apart from gauge, to those working on the Southern Railway of England at that time. The Pullman car supplement, over and above the third class fare and the cost of any meals or drink purchased, was 1s (5p) for 50 miles. Whether a passenger from Dublin to Mullingar (a distance of 50¼ miles) got away with paying one shilling or was charged double that amount, I cannot say.

There was no catering on the night Mails – one brought one's own or tightened one's belt as the clock crept closer and closer to midnight and the train rattled on into the western night between lengthy stops at Kiltoom,

Knockcroghery, Roscommon, Donamon, Ballymoe, Castlerea, Ballinlough, Ballyhaunis, Bekan, Claremorris, Balla, Manulla, Castlebar, Islandeady, Westport, Newport and Mallarany. Truly, Achill was a long way from Dublin!

Of the trains just mentioned, I saw only the 14.45 (though not everyday), the down night Mail and the up day Mail. However, it was on the 14.45 train that one day I saw No 7 *Connemara* in its full glory as a Midland engine, and not as an anonymous grey Great Southern wraith, number five hundred and forty something. I have earlier mentioned the six-wheeler at the head of that train, the probable reason for remembering which was that one of its compartments was labelled 'Ladies Only', something I had never seen before. Whether this was because no ladies, as distinct from mere women, ever travelled on the Great Northern or the Dublin and South Eastern, or because those who did were made of sterner stuff than their Midland and Western sisters, and could be relied upon to give any predatory male his due desserts, I cannot say.

GSWR 0-4-4BT No 83 was built in 1884 at Inchicore and is seen as built. The designation 'BT' stood for 'back tank', an unusual arrangement. An engine of this class worked the Banagher to Clara branch in 1926. No 83 was withdrawn in 1928, officially designated E3 class.

Real Photographs 87076, courtesy CP Friel

There was an occasion, however, when my mother would have been glad of 'ladies only' accommodation on the Ballina branch train. On a night in 1914 or 1915 she travelled from Manulla in the company of a man, a total stranger, in an unlighted non-corridor compartment. She was travelling to Ballina (I never thought to ask her did she change compartments at Ballyvary or Foxford) and that journey made a lifelong impression on her. Need I say that she suffered no harm? Probably the man was as anxious as she was.

I once had a minor adventure myself involving a 'ladies only' compartment. In the spring of 1933, staying with an uncle and aunt in a south London suburb, I was returning to their house from the city at the peak of the evening rush hour. I was just, and only just, in time to hurl myself into a rear compartment of an over full commuter train which was on the point of starting from the Brighton section of Victoria station. After I had regained by breath, and glanced around at my tightly packed fellow passengers, it occurred to me that there were a lot of women present; a second glance revealed that except for myself there were no men; and a third provided the information that according to the sticker on a quarter light (which I read backwards with some difficulty and mounting embarrassment), I was in a 'ladies only' compartment. At the first stop I beat an ignominious retreat to a compartment further up the train. As a callow and innocent Irish 18-year-old, I certainly did not have the moral courage to sit the journey out among the cockney Amazons.

But we have come a long way from Mullingar. The up day and down night Mails were the trains I saw every day, as well as the Clara branch mixed and the down evening Cavan passenger. Let us take a look at the two mainline trains in the order in which I have mentioned them.

At around 17.40 each evening the Banagher/Clara mixed would appear at the up main platform headed by its ex-GSWR 0-4-4T. The passenger section of this train consisted of two six-wheelers, and behind them would be goods wagons and a brake van. Presumably, as well as Clara and Horseleap goods traffic, these latter vehicles would have included pickups from Castletown and Streamstown. Similarly among the few passengers detraining at Mullingar there would be human pickups from the same two small stations, thus enabling the Mail to run non-stop from Moate to Mullingar. I once, but only once, saw a passenger get out of a first class compartment of the branch train. If he had got on at Horseleap, he was no doubt considered as the next best thing to a corpse. Soon after arrival of the 'Clara', the diminutive engine would back its train out to the sidings at the west end of the station, and at about the time this manoeuvre was in progress, or a little later, the up Sligo train would arrive at its platform on the north side of the station. The locomotive would be a 4-4-0, usually one of the smaller Cusack type, whilst the train consisted of a six-wheeled combined guards brake and TPO (an intriguing vehicle for anyone reared on GNR(I) bogie carriages), followed by two bogie corridor coaches and finally a six-wheeled brake. Immediately on arrival the train would be divided behind the TPO and the engine would take the latter away to the bay platform (the rails of which have now been lifted). The coast was now clear for the arrival of the main section of the Mail, which event occurred at about 17.55. The latter train, even without the Sligo portion, was an impressive sight to my eyes, accustomed, so far as Ireland was concerned, to trains no larger than the Wexford Mails or the Rosslares. In my recollection the engine was more often a rebuilt large Cusack 4-4-0 than a 'Woolwich', though the latter engines did take their turn on the Mails. Behind the locomotive was the bogie TPO, No 1m, followed by the solid and imposing clerestory-roofed semi-open first class coach built in the early years of the

GSR No 377 of Class K1, one of the original (MGWR) 'Woolwich' 2-6-0s, approaching Mullingar on a down express. The down main platform at Mullingar was little used after the diversion of the Galway and Mayo trains to the old GSWR route between Dublin and Athlone. That was was where the author saw Midland Great Western Class 'C' 4-4-0 Connemara at the head of a Galway train, the first carriage of which was a six-wheeler with 'Ladies Only' compartments.

Kelland Collection 23148, courtesy CP Friel

century. Behind the first was the very similar looking centre-kitchen dining car, built at the same time as the first. Somewhat surprisingly, the diner bore the same number, 1m, as the TPO. When I first saw these two vehicles in 1926 my 11-year-old brain was puzzled – it took a while to work out that the MGWR numbered dining cars and TPOs in separate series. Behind the dining car were two thirds, most probably ex-MGWR, but my memory is not too clear on this. The sixth and last vehicle of this first (Galway) section of the Mail was a bogie brake. Finally, at the tail of the train, came a bogie from Ballina and a bogie and six-wheeled van from Achill. This train too would, on arrival at Mullingar, be hooked off immediately behind its TPO, after which the engine and latter vehicle would draw ahead and set back against the two bogies and van from Sligo. After the Sligo line Mails had been transferred to TPO No 1m, the big engine brought the four vehicles out towards Dublin and again set back, this time against the first

class carriage of the Galway/Mayo train. The next and final procedure before departure was to take water, after which the long train, ten bogies and two six-wheeled vans, set out on its not too arduous journey to Broadstone, a distance of 50¼ miles, scheduled for 75 minutes, equating to an average speed of 40 mph. Taking account of the 4-4-0s, and making every allowance for the restricted curves, this timing can scarcely have extended the 'Woolwichs'.

On Friday evenings there was an additional train to be seen, the 'Mayo Mail'. I do not know if that was ever the train's official designation but it was the term used by a driver when, with great daring, I asked him if the train was a special. I still remember the exact words of his reply: "This is the Mayo Mail, run special every Friday." But what was this train with the important sounding name – did it carry identically numbered TPO and dining car to confuse a juvenile admirer or did a shining 'Woolwich', or a 'Celtic' still wearing its

GSR J5 0-6-0 No 642 was one of the 'mixed traffics' (Class 'F') of the former MGWR. Some of these engines were built at the company's Broadstone works, and the rest at Newcastle-on-Tyne by Armstrong Whitworth. There were 23 in all, built between 1921 and 1924. The only noticeable difference between the two batches was that the Broadstone engines had raised footplating, to give access to the coupling rod crank pins, while the 'Tynesiders' had oiling crescents in the splashers.

Real Photographs, courtesy CP Friel

MGWR livery, head its long line of corridor bogies? Far from it, although the engine I recall on this train was reasonably impressive – a 'mixed traffic', one of the large wheeled 0-6-0s with high-pitched boilers, known by the GSR as the 623 class.

The 'mixed traffics' were genuine Midland Great Western locomotives, the last class to be designed and built at Broadstone (the first twelve 'Woolwichs' were only erected there). The one on the Mayo Mail had a genuine Midland Great Western train behind it, six-wheelers one and all, whose rooftop lamp housings reached scarcely as high as the top of the engine cab. There may have been a few examples of that Midland speciality – the lavatory carriage – among them, but I cannot be sure of this. The majority of passengers from Newport, Bekan, Balinlough and other long-closed stations no doubt had to endure several hours of lavatoryless, jerky progress,

sitting upright on hard, thinly upholstered seats in compartments whose partitions, in many cases, reached only to shoulder height. In late summer many of the travellers would be seasonal agricultural workers, on their way to the Holyhead and Liverpool boats and thence to employment in the British corn and potato fields.

Whether the main up Mail or the Mayo Mail ran through to Dun Laoghaire pier in 1926 and 1927, I cannot be certain. I do know that in 1925 my mother and one of my brothers travelled directly from the pier to the west in the regular down Mail. Certainly in 1930, or thereabouts, the up Mail did not run to the pier, as I remember being at Broadstone one summer evening to meet my father coming from Athlone, when a short train of six-wheelers was used to bring Mail passengers down to the pier. At least some of these six-wheelers were painted in the recently introduced brown and cream colour. On this particular evening (probably a Saturday) there was no Mayo Mail, as a large number of seasonal workers emerged from the mainline train and boarded the one for the pier. It must have been at more or less the same time as this Broadstone visit that I made my first acquaintance with the GSWR (other than seeing the horse boxes and six-wheeled brake vans at Sutton), as I remember again meeting my father coming from Athlone, but this time at Kingsbridge. However, it was to be several years before I made any meaningful contact with the Southern.

Just as the appearance of the Banagher and Clara branch train was the prelude to the arrival of the up Mail at Mullingar, so the down evening Cavan train served as a harbinger of the down night Mail. The Cavan train was vintage MGWR throughout – the motive power was an Atock 2-4-0 in original

condition, and in 1926 still carrying its nameplate and MGWR-lettered tender. All three or four coaches were usually six-wheelers, and there would be a tail of one or more four-wheeled fitted vans. Few passengers alighted from the Cavan train at Mullingar and it is to be hoped that reasonable numbers used the intermediate stations onwards from Dublin. However, the train served a useful purpose for Mullingar in that it brought the Dublin evening papers, in those days the *Herald* and the *Mail*, the former of which is still with us, the latter long since extinct. After the few passengers had disembarked, the papers and parcels had been unloaded and the engine had taken water, the train departed for Inny Junction (stopping at Clonhugh and Multyfarnham), there to be overtaken by the down Sligo night Mail, out of which it provided a connection to Cavan and intermediate stations.

MGWR 2-4-0 Aurora *which, with one or two other 'Midland' engines, spent some time on Dublin, Bray and Greystones local trains in the early days after the 1925 amalgamation. She is pictured here on a Dublin–Cavan train at Mullingar in 1926. Note the later style of MGWR cab.*

JE Kide, courtesy CP Friel

The night Mail ex-Broadstone would be headed by a Cusack 4-4-0 or a 'Woolwich', immediately behind which came a six-wheeled TPO, followed by the Galway coaches and those for Sligo on the tail of the train. The Mail halted outside the station, just to the east of the divergence of the main and Sligo lines, where the Sligo vehicles would be uncoupled. The Galway train then came in to the down main platform, after which the Sligo engine, which had been standing at the down branch platform, backed out and collected its train. Apart from the fact that the TPO was a six-wheeler and not a bogie vehicle, I can remember very little about the make-up of the main portion of the night Mail or of the Sligo section, and there was a very good reason for this which even now, almost 75 years later, I recall with pleasure. In the summer of 1927, roughly two years after my first footplate trips running round the Howth branch train, I had my second series of locomotive rides. During this visit to Mullingar there was a driver on the Sligo night Mail turn who understood the aspirations of a 12-year-old standing silent but ever hopeful beside his engine. In short, at least twice, and I rather think three times, I was invited on to the engine for the run out to the Sligo coaches and back again with them to the platform. Small wonder that I had no eye for the composition of the trains in 1927, and that the recollection of this early footplating extinguished almost everything I might otherwise have remembered about the format of the night Mails the year before. I do recall, however, that the Sligo train (contrary to the practice with the day service) did not have a TPO, and that in 1927 the locomotive was painted in Great Southern style.

Before leaving the trains of the South Eastern and Midland sections of the GSR, I should perhaps say something about the livery of the passenger stock in the 1920s and early 1930s.

When I first got to know Bray and the neighbouring stations, virtually all coaches were painted in the colours of their former owners.

Very soon, however, the overall bluish purple of the Great Southern and Western, continued by the GSR, began to be applied to the Midland Great Western and Dublin and South Eastern carriages. This was followed, from about 1930, by a change to the two-tone colour scheme somewhat reminiscent of that of the English Great Western and already mentioned in connection with the Broadstone–Dun Laoghaire pier train. For a while in 1928, when a very intensive suburban service was introduced on the coast line of the South Eastern, a number of six-wheelers were running painted in grey undercoating only, albeit with the normal transferred numbers, coats of arms and class designations.

As with Bray so with Mullingar, though there were no grey horrors to be seen at the latter place. In 1926 there was still some Midland Great Western painting around, but by the following year the Inchicore purple was taking over fast. In the 1930s, as for instance when I observed the up Mail at Broadstone, the brown and cream was well in evidence. Brown (or rather chocolate) and cream were also the Pullman colours. My recollection is that after the Pullman cars on the GSR were acquired by the railway company, and were designated 'Great Southern Railways Pullmans', they retained their original colours for some time, eventually passing straight from chocolate and cream to CIÉ green. I have already mentioned that these cars, apart from their bogies, were identical to those working on the Southern Railway of England. A drawing which I obtained from the Pullman Car Company many years ago, and which is now in the Irish Railway Record Society archives, is lettered 'Southern Railway' in large block capitals, and in smaller letters immediately above these, and obviously stuck on as an afterthought, 'Ireland'. Do we detect here the malign influence of some xenophobic Englishman who was determined that if his country's Southern was not 'Great', Ireland's similarly named railway should not be either?

3 Early Irish Mainline Journeys

This chapter deals with my earliest memories of Irish mainline journeys. At the age of one or two I travelled between Dublin and Ballina, return each time, the Midland thus beating the Northern by 12 years for the honour of transporting me on my first long-distance Irish journey, but I cannot claim to remember anything of these early trips. Indeed, I do not remember a very great deal about the journeys on the GNR(I), DSER and MGWR lines about to be described, but perhaps my sketchy recollections of rail travel more than 70 years ago may be of some interest – after all, I doubt if the majority of readers (or even some of their parents) were born by 1928 or 1930.

Despite the increasing variety of my train watching from 1925 onwards, and in particular my growing knowledge of mainline services, it was not until 1928 that I made my first remembered Irish mainline journey. In view of my early, and subsequently lifelong, interest in the Great Northern (and my close acquaintance with the Portadown–Derry section many years later), it was wholly appropriate that this journey should have been from Strabane to Dublin.

During the Easter holidays of 1928 I spent some time with my father in County Donegal. We travelled from Dublin by car, the long way round via Sligo, taking about six hours to get to the latter town from our house in Shankill, and another two or so on to Mount Charles, our first place of call. Here I may note a non-railway event, still clearly remembered. It was at Mount Charles in the spring of 1928 that I heard that the first successful non-stop east to west crossing of the Atlantic by air had been made, from Portmarnock Strand to Greenley Island, Labrador, by a German machine crewed by two Germans, Baron von Huenfield

and Captain Kohl, and Colonel Fitzmaurice of the Irish Army Air Corps.

Although we stayed at various places which had County Donegal or Lough Swilly stations, ending up in Buncrana, from where we went to both Moville and Strabane, I cannot remember seeing one narrow gauge loco, let alone a train, though I must surely have seen the CDR in action at Strabane. Maybe things might have been different had we stayed in Stranorlar. In April 1925, when my mother and one of my brothers accompanied my father to County Donegal, my brother spent more than one evening at Stranorlar station; since he was only six years of age it was deemed appropriate for him to be accompanied by his mother on his station visits. The story goes that mother and son were sitting one evening on the platform contemplating a train that seemed to be making an unduly long wait. After some time a railway official approached them and politely asked would they mind taking their seats, as the train was overdue for departure; where it was bound for I do not know, possibly the Glenties branch. As a postscript to this CDR interpolation, I can mention that the only time I remember seeing a Donegal locomotive before 1937 was at Rossnowlagh in 1924 – the engine was old No 6, *Columkille*, a 4-6-0T. It was also in 1924 that I had my first sight of SLNCR motive power. This was at Colloney, but all I remember is that the machine was a tank loco (not very surprising) and that it was in the charge of a friendly driver who cheerfully answered my many questions.

It is time to get back to the Great Northern, by courtesy of which company I returned from County Donegal. I travelled from Strabane by the Mail, which left Derry at 16:10 and connected into the up Dublin Mail at

Portadown. My first impressions of long-distance GNR(I) travel were twofold: first, I thought that the standard of comfort provided for third class passengers was fairly basic; and second, that the trains showed a fair turn of speed. As regards comfort, the Great Northern's wooden mainline stock of the period, though much of it was recently built, certainly offered no superfluous luxury to third class passengers. Coaches were centre corridor with thinly upholstered wooden seats, accommodating three on one side and two on the other. There were nine sections, and one toilet compartment, per coach; doors were provided in alternate sections, but the non-door sections had traditional quarter lights, with drop lights between these, exactly as if they also had doors. Floors were often bare boards, though sometimes there was linoleum covering. This all added up to a pretty cheerless sort of vehicle, but one must not forget that until the advent of the first AEC railcars in 1950 the GNR(I) provided three classes of accommodation in all trains (small railcars and railbuses excepted). At the time of which I am writing, the blue upholstered seats and the mats (with the company's coat of arms woven into their fabric) on the lino-covered floors of the second class accommodation provided very reasonable facilities for travellers, which were certainly as superior to the best third class of the Midland Great Western as the latter was to the third of the Northern. Whether it was more or less of an ordeal to travel in a full MGWR third class six-wheeler than in a full GNR(I) 100-seater non-corridor bogie probably depended upon which vehicle one had last been in – the one further back in the memory was automatically the better.

As regards my second impression – speed – Great Northern trains were fast by Irish standards, though not as fast on the main line as they became a few years later (Derry Road timings were already about as tight as was practicable). I have no doubt that my enduring impression of fast travel on both sections of the journey was partly due to the high proportion of short rails. Writing with the hindsight engendered by numerous journeys on the Derry Road in later years, I am certain that for a 13-year-old, inexperienced in mainline travel, the mixture of short rails, less than glass-smooth track and a real speed of about 60 mph down Pomeroy bank provided a convincing sensation of very rapid progress. Much the same could be said of the descent of the Wellington bank towards Dundalk, where the better condition of the track would have been counterbalanced by the considerably higher real speed. Even as late as 1939 there were short rails between Adavoyle and Mount Pleasant.

During the first stage of the journey I expended the sum of ten 'old pence', about 4p, on what was known as a 'plain tea'. I will have more to say about railway catering services later, but perhaps a brief description of how Great Northern travellers in the 1920s negotiated their plain teas may be interesting here. Until 1936 there were no buffet cars on the 09.15 and 15.15 down and 10.30 and 14.45 up mainline expresses. However, so-called 'tea cars' were incorporated in the make-up of these trains as they were in some of the Belfast–Derry (and later Belfast–Cavan) ones also.

The construction of a tea car was scarcely an arduous feat of mechanical engineering. The seats were removed from one section or compartment of a standard third, and simple storage, water heating and other facilities were installed. From this base a single male or female attendant dispensed, at the aforesaid price of tenpence, trays which held a pot of tea, milk, biscuits, bread and jam and a small slice of slab cake. The passenger balanced the tray as best as he or she could – on the empty seat beside him or her (if lucky), or otherwise on the knees. No doubt the latter alternative produced a few spills on the ferocious curves

This 1952 picture shows rebuilt Class PPs 4-4-0 No 44 of the GNR(I) shunting at Omagh, the junction of the 'Irish North' and the 'Derry Road.' The engine is on the former line, the Derry Road diverging to the left of the cabin. The passenger station was immediately behind the photographer. The concrete edging of the ramp from the down through platform is just visible in front of No 44's bogie wheels.

WT Scott

between Dungannon and Omagh; curves to which many drivers were not inclined to afford the full respect laid down in the working timetables and their appendices, and of which they (the drivers) were reminded by the rectangular advance warning boards with their red relief lettering. These boards warned, 'Reduce speed to __ miles per hour' and were followed by smaller boards announcing, for example, '30 C', followed in due course by '30 T'. Possibly, on my journey from Strabane the driver conscientiously observed all restrictions. At any rate I do not remember spilling my tea, nor seeing anyone else do so either.

Anyway, spartan third class accommodation and rapid, if scarcely smooth, progress got us to Portadown, behind what is

remembered as a black 4-4-0. This is likely to have been a newly rebuilt Q, but at that time I was not sufficiently well informed on GNR(I) engines to be able to identify it. Where the loco, whatever its type, differed from what would have been seen a few years later was that instead of the letters 'GNR' on its tender, the words 'Great Northern' appeared in full, as they did also on the sides of tank engines of the period.

My lack of extensive knowledge of the Northern, outside of the Howth branch, showed itself on arrival at Portadown. Due to the lack of books on Irish railways, I had no idea of the layout of the junction. However, from my 13-year-old knowledge of geography, I knew that to travel from Strabane to Dublin one went in a southerly direction, and that the same applied to Dublin from Belfast. I must therefore have assumed that we arrived in Portadown from Strabane still travelling south, so imagine my surprise when, after getting out of the Derry train and waiting for a short while, I beheld the Dublin train travelling in what I assumed to be a northerly direction. This sounds rather infantile, but at the time I suffered a very confused few minutes.

However, I boarded the Dublin train – more basic wooden thirds and another black 4-4-0 – and presumably soon managed to reorientate myself. I do not remember much detail of the journey from Portadown to Dublin except for a general impression of speed (after all this was the Mail), but at Dundalk I made my first contact on a railway journey with those invariable adjuncts to cross-border travel – customs officers. I had bought a small bag of grain (food for my pet mice) in Moville that morning, and at Dundalk a customs man displayed what I thought was a quite unwarranted curiosity about it. Whatever my lack of knowledge of Portadown, my grasp of the overall economic and political geography of Ireland was quite sufficient for me to know that the passage of my parcel of mouse food from Moville to Dublin constituted what I later learned was designated by the GNR(I) as 'Free to Free' traffic (ie from one area of the then Irish Free State to another via Northern Ireland), and as such did not attract any customs duties or prohibitions.

So much for my first acquaintance with Great Northern mainlines – and it was 'lines' rather than 'line', for it was always maintained at Amiens Street that Portadown–Derry, though obviously not *the*, was *a* main line. We must now return to the South Eastern. In August 1930, I travelled from Bray to Wexford by my old friend the 10.30 from Harcourt Street. Little had changed since I had first seen this train almost five years earlier. The small ex-DSER 4-4-0; the two bogies plus six-

wheeled brake; and the fitted vans were just as I remembered them, though there were no longer any DSER liveries on either engine or coaching vehicles. Not that DSER paint would ever have adorned the carriage in which I travelled, an ex-MGWR open third with reversible tramcar pattern seats, which always remained in my mind as being covered with a sort of basket work. This lasting memory of a most unusual type of railway carriage upholstery was confirmed when I read Mr P O'Cuimin's article on MGWR carriage stock in the June and October 1971 issues of the *Journal of the Irish Railway Record Society*. The article related how MGWR bogie third No 83 was, at some time between 1916 and 1918, given a new centre corridor body with reversible seats, and that these seats were finished in rattan. After more than 40 years of memory of this unusual vehicle, it was almost like meeting an old friend to find it illustrated in Mr O'Cuimin's article. As compared to the Great Northern centre corridor coaches in which I had travelled two years previously, No 83 had, for the most part, wide windows between each pair of seats.

Although I had never been in Wexford before 1930, I had earlier travelled by rail as far as Wicklow. In the summer of 1928 a group from my school in Bray travelled, by the 10.30, for the annual picnic to the Silver Strand, south of Wicklow. This outing is worth mentioning because we travelled in a private saloon, such vehicles still being available for party use. The saloon was a six-wheeler, but I am not sure as to what company it originated from. My admittedly hazy memory says "Great Southern and Western", but with no great degree of conviction. After we had detrained at Wicklow, the train engine shunted the saloon into a siding on the down side of the line. Presumably the delay thus caused was accepted stoically by the passengers remaining in the train – with 17 intermediate stops between Bray and Wexford, those of them who were regular travellers must have long since become accustomed to late arrivals. Passengers by the up Mail were better treated, however – on our return by that latter train we had to dispose ourselves throughout the ordinary accommodation as best we could, leaving our luxurious private vehicle still in its siding. It was probably regard for the Mail connections, rather than for the passengers, that precluded our finishing our journey as it had begun. The track layout at Wicklow, too, would have made a 'pick-up' of the saloon rather difficult.

I had a second and much longer trip on the South Eastern up Mail when I returned from my visit to Wexford in 1930. My main recollection of this journey is that of sampling the provisions in one of the already mentioned old Great Southern and Western diners. I doubt if I got a plain tea for ten pence, but the surroundings in which I consumed my meal were much more convenient and comfortable than those experienced when eating from a tray in an ordinary Great Northern third class carriage. However, since the DSER Mail diner had been built in 1898 as a first class for service in the Dublin–Cork Mail set, its wide fixed-seats and generous leg room were only to be expected.

The only other Irish non-suburban rail journeys which I made before moving to Scotland in 1933 were two on the Midland – one right through on the Mail from Ballina to Broadstone and one to Ballina from Mullingar by the down day Mail. Both of these trips took place in 1931, and as regards the up Mail there was no obvious change from the conditions which obtained in 1926 and 1927, including the through coaches from both Achill and the Ballina branch. I remember the journey because from Manulla to Athlone the loco was an 'Achill bogie', one of the small ex-MGWR 4-4-0s which had been rebuilt around 1900 from a class of 2-4-0s dating from 1880. (The well-known standard 2-4-0s came out in 1893) The other MGWR journey which I made in 1931 provided evidence that the Great Southern Railways, despite growing bus competition, either did not appreciate the need to provide attractive through services between Dublin and Co Mayo, or did not have the vehicles with which to operate them. To travel from Mullingar (or Dublin) to Ballina by the first available service of the day entailed two changes of train, at Athlone and Manulla, finishing the journey in a six-wheeler with a limited number of full-height partitions between compartments. I rather think that the train from Athlone to Manulla (and onwards to Castlebar, Westport and Achill) was also composed of six-wheeled stock. Motive power on the Ballina branch was one of the ubiquitous standard 2-4-0s on each of the journeys just mentioned. While on the subject of 2-4-0s, an abiding memory dating from 1924, and stemming from one of our annual journeys to the south of England, was of the ex-LNWR 'Precedent' class *Merrie Carlisle* in Crewe station, painted in the full Midland red colour which not long afterwards became restricted on the LMS to the larger passenger locomotives only.

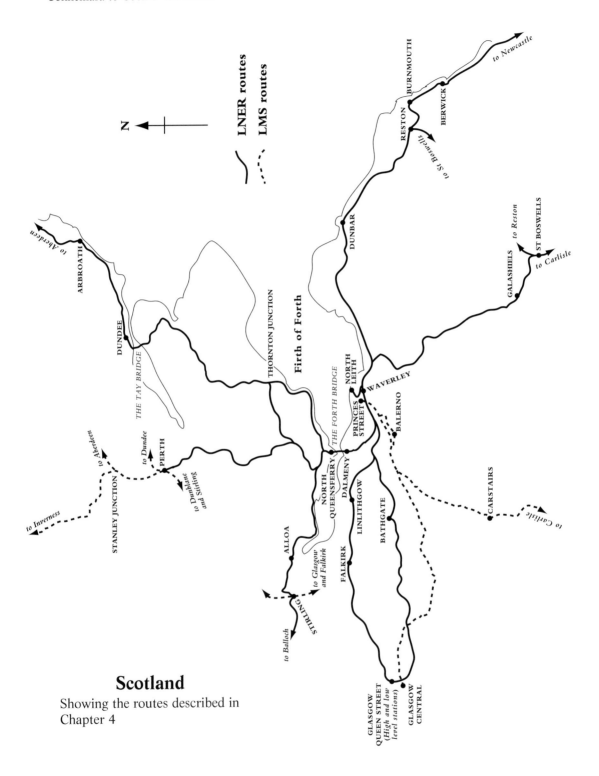

LNER routes

LMS routes

N

to Newcastle

BURNMOUTH

RESTON

BERWICK

to St Boswells

DUNBAR

to Reston

GALASHIELS   ST BOSWELLS

to Carlisle

to Aberdeen

ARBROATH

DUNDEE

THE TAY BRIDGE

THORNTON JUNCTION

Firth of Forth

NORTH LEITH

WAVERLEY

PRINCES STREET

BALERNO

to Aberdeen

to Dundee

PERTH

STANLEY JUNCTION

to Dunblane and Stirling

to Inverness

NORTH QUEENSFERRY

THE FORTH BRIDGE

DALMENY

LINLITHGOW

BATHGATE

CARSTAIRS

to Carlisle

ALLOA

to Glasgow and Falkirk

FALKIRK

to Balloch

STIRLING

GLASGOW QUEEN STREET
(High and low level stations)

GLASGOW CENTRAL

Scotland

Showing the routes described in
Chapter 4

4 Scottish Interlude

My railway experience broadened considerably after the summer of 1933, for at the end of July of that year our family moved to Edinburgh, where we lived for the next four years.

I had already been in Scotland for a short holiday in 1928, travelling by 'long sea' from Dublin to Glasgow, and thence by LMS rail (Caledonian section) onwards to Edinburgh. A comparatively short journey from Edinburgh to Dunbar, about 30 miles from the former city on the East Coast Main Line, remains firmly in my recollection. The reason is that this was the only time I saw one of the GCR 'Director' class 4-4-0s in LNER green livery. The train on which I travelled from Edinburgh came through from Glasgow. It was indeed the one-time celebrated Glasgow–Leeds 'Diner' – a fact which I did not realise until five years later after residence in Edinburgh had familiarised me with the more important passenger workings on the North British section of the London and North Eastern.

This Glasgow–Leeds train had achieved fame in the early years of the century when it was booked to average just over 61 mph start to stop between Darlington and York, at a time when mile-a-minute timings were rare in Britain. When introduced, this was the fastest train in England. When one thinks of high-speed British trains between 1900 and the 'Grouping', it is generally the Great Western and the Great Northern (England) companies that come to mind. It is interesting, therefore, that this Darlington–York example of fast running was provided by the North Eastern. Whether one can trace any direct connection between high speeds on the North Eastern of England before 1914 and George Glover's contribution to the spectacular accelerations

on the Great Northern of Ireland, some 20 years later, is open to debate. But certainly the inter-war Mechanical Engineer of the latter company had been reared in the right tradition.

The 'Director' which I saw bringing the Glasgow–Leeds train into the long through platform on the south side of the Waverley station in Edinburgh would have come off there, and a North Eastern section engine would have taken the train on to Dunbar and beyond. In 1928 this latter engine was quite likely an ex-North Eastern 'Atlantic', though in later years a Gresley 'Pacific' was standard motive power south of Edinburgh. Changing engines on southbound East Coast trains (from Glasgow or Aberdeen) dated back to pre-Grouping days when the North Eastern provided the motive power for express workings south of Edinburgh, even though the meeting point of NBR and NER was at Berwick, some 57 miles beyond the Scottish capital.

The 'Director' which I saw in 1928 would have been one of the batch built about 1925, specifically for service in Scotland, and which differed from the original Great Central type in having side-window cabs and shorter chimneys and domes, to fit the NBR loading gauge. Although this engine was painted green in 1928, it would shortly afterwards have lost its express passenger livery in favour of the black paint to which all of the class, and many other passenger types on both LNER and LMS, were relegated in the late 1920s and early 1930s. It was particularly the numerous 4-4-0 classes which suffered in this way. So far as I can remember, of all the 4-4-0s only the 'Shires' and 'Hunts' on the LNER and the Midland 'Compounds' on the LMS continued to be painted green and red respectively.

I have said that the Glasgow–Leeds 'Diner' arrived at the long through platform on the south side of Waverley station, Edinburgh. This was interesting in that it involved bringing in an up through train on the down through road. Why this was so I never discovered. Whether the 'Director' ex-Glasgow was replaced by an 'Atlantic' or a 'Pacific' I do not remember; I had already seen one of the latter engines at the Wembley Exhibition in 1924. For me, at the age of nine, LNER No 4472, the *Flying Scotsman*, was the highlight of the entire exhibition. Also seen were GWR *Caerphilly Castle* and an LMS machine painted red and named *Prince of Wales*. (This was a unique locomotive – a 'Prince of Wales' class 4-6-0 built new in 1924 by Beardmore with outside Walschaerts valve gear driving inside valves, and temporarily named for the Wembley Exhibition.) During the four years I lived in Edinburgh the Gresley 'Pacifics' multiplied in Scotland, and it was during that time that there appeared not only the last of the 'conventional' type but also the first of the A4 streamlined series.

Waverley station in the 1930s was a train watcher's delight. The actual station was not particularly well laid out for observation of engines and coaches, as it was too large to see everything that was going on at any one time. However, there was a footpath in Princes Street Gardens through which the main line to Glasgow, Perth and Aberdeen ran in a cutting, just at the west end of the station, from which a superb view could be obtained. Since the main suburban service was over a circular route, and since some of the stopping trains for the Dunbar and Berwick directions towards the east started their journeys at Corstorphine in the western suburbs, one saw from the path in the gardens a very large proportion of all the movements into and out of the station. For good measure Haymarket shed, the more important of the two which supplied motive power for the Waverley trains, was to the west of the station, which enabled one to observe light engine movements as well as train arrivals and departures. The second shed was Saint Margaret's which occupied the site of the original workshops of the North British Railway, some distance to the east of the station.

When I came to Edinburgh in 1933 the imposing former North British 'Atlantics' were still common. They regularly worked express services to Carlisle over the difficult 'Waverley route', and also to Aberdeen. One saw them less often on Glasgow and Perth trains. Trains could load up to 12 bogies on the Aberdeen road and up to ten to Carlisle, in which cases pilots would be needed. In accordance with the old North British custom, assisting locomotives were always placed behind the train engines, the reason being to ensure that the booked train driver, and not the pilot driver, was in charge of the brake.

One is reminded of the regulations of the GNR(I) and GSWR in Ireland (but not, I think, the MGWR), that where a 'goods engine', so described in the GNR(I) regulation, was coupled with a passenger engine, the former had always to be next to the train. The Great Northern regulation also stipulated that in such circumstances the speed must "be regulated to suit the goods engine". Since on the GNR(I) a goods engine was always a 0-6-0, this latter precept conjures up the bizarre picture of an S class on a heavy southbound mainline express, assisted from Goraghwood by a PG, tearing down through Mount Pleasant with the crew of the latter engine blowing fanfares on the whistle in a vain attempt to intimate to the driver of the 4-4-0 that the speed did not suit the goods engine. A fantasy, the reader may say, but I have 'chapter and verse' for an actual event not all that different. Nearly 40 years ago, a Portadown driver told me that in his firing days he and his mate were once called on to pilot a 'Compound' from Portadown to Dundalk. Their engine was a 4-4-2T, and hence not required to be between

LNER 'Atlantic' No 9509 (formerly North British No 509 Duke of Rothesay*). This loco and sister engine No 9510 (North British No 510), which were built in 1920, were the last of the 22 North British 'Atlantics', 14 of which entered service in 1906, and a further six in 1910. Compared to these 20 locos, the* Duke of Rothesay *and the* Lord Provost *had larger cylinders and were superheated, standards to which the other engines were rebuilt. These big 4-4-2s worked expresses on the Aberdeen, Carlisle, and Glasgow roads, but towards the end of the 1930s withdrawal started. By the end of World War Two, they had all gone.*

Historical Model Railway Society AAH928

the big 'Compound' and its train. It was arranged between the crew of the pilot and the Dundalk men on the train engine that once they had reached the top of the bank south of Bessbrook the tank engine could be shut off, and that on the run down towards Dundalk any power required would be supplied by the 'Compound'. Unfortunately for the Portadown men, the Dundalk driver was one of the old school who believed in steaming his engine down through Adavoyle and Mount Pleasant, not shutting off until the last possible moment allowed for, before stopping at Dundalk. My informant said that he had never been so terrified in his life, being convinced that at any moment the little tank engine would roll clean off the track. However, this chapter is supposed to relate primarily to Scotland, so let us leave the Wellington bank and return to the North British.

The custom of putting the train engine in front of the pilot ensured that on a summer evening one might see the Aberdeen connection off the down 'Flying Scotsman', or its relief, starting from Waverley with a large green 'Atlantic' at its head, followed by a small black ex-NBR 4-4-0 (about the size of a rebuilt GSWR 60 class) which was coupled to the leading train vehicle. Other and larger types of ex-NBR 4-4-0s, including the 'Scotts' and 'Glens', were also used as pilots, and also ex-Great Northern Ivatt machines, several of which were shedded at Haymarket. The combination of a large 'Atlantic' and a small 4-4-0 looked unbalanced. The effect was not so marked if the leading engine was a 'Shire' (three-cylinder 4-4-0) or a 'Director', but it was bizarre in the extreme when, as was occasionally the case, a 'Pacific' needed a pilot.

There were other 'Pacifics' around as well

Former North British Railway 'Scott' class 4-4-0 No 359 (LNER D29 No 9359) Dirck Hatteraick *in early LNER days, when engine numbers were shown on the tenders. This class, of which there were a total of 16, dated from 1909, although 359 first entered service in 1911. These locos were not superheated until after the Grouping.*

Historical Model Railway Society AAC712

LNER D30 class 4-4-0 No 9426 Norna, *(NBR 'Enlarged Scott' No 426). These locos were superheated from the start, and had larger cylinders (20"x 26") than the original 'Scotts'. They worked all sorts of passenger trains all over the North British system, and were also to be seen on the NER Newcastle to Carlisle line, having worked in from Hawick via Riccarton Junction. The author's first journey over the LNER main line from Edinburgh to Glasgow was made behind No 9497 of this class,* Peter Poundtext.

Historical Model Railway Society ACW501

LNER C7 class 'Atlantic' loco No 735 (ex-NER 'Z' class). On these 3-cylinder machines, all cylinders drove on to the leading coupled axle.

Historical Model Railway Society ACW208

One of the two former North Eastern Railway C7 'Atlantics' which were rebuilt by Gresley in 1931 to Class C9 with booster fitted rear bogies, to which the tenders (not the original vehicles) were articulated. According to the late OS Nock, Gresley considered 'boosterising' a number of these locos in order to provide reserve power for Anglo-Scottish expresses north of York. However, no more 'Z' class engines were converted, nor did similar experimental work on an ex-Great Northern (England) 4-4-2 lead to any long-term results.

Historical Model Railway Society ACW209

as Gresley's. From time to time one of the long North Eastern type, with outside connecting rods driving on to the leading pair of coupled wheels, but with inside valve gear, would appear on its way to or from Haymarket shed after or before working an East Coast express or (more usually) semi-fast. These engines had six-wheeled tenders which, matched with long engines, gave an unbalanced appearance. Other long North Eastern engines were the three-cylinder Class 'Z' 'Atlantics', again with drive to the leading coupled wheels. Up to about the end of 1935 these were fairly common, sometimes working in pairs between Newcastle and Edinburgh. Two of these machines were reconstructed by Gresley, the design incorporating a four-wheeled bogie behind the drivers, to which locomotive and tender were articulated, and to which there was 'booster' drive. I saw one of these locos a couple of times. The North Eastern two-cylinder 'Atlantics', with drive on the second pair of coupled wheels, were only occasional visitors to Edinburgh in my time.

I could continue in this fashion for a long time, since there were so many classes of engine to be seen at Waverley 60 odd years ago; however, so as not to bore readers, I will complete my survey of LNER passenger engines at Edinburgh by listing the main services which I most regularly saw operating, and the engines most commonly used on these.

The important East Coast expresses to Newcastle and beyond, including the summer non-stop 'Flying Scotsman', were almost entirely the preserve of the Gresley 'Pacifics'. Other trains to Newcastle might have 'Pacifics' of either GNR or NER design, or NER 'Atlantics'. Occasionally I saw the experimental high pressure 4-6-4 No 10000 – once or twice it was working the Glasgow–Leeds 'Diner'. Stopping trains southwards to Berwick (the meeting point of the former North Eastern and North British companies) usually had ex-NBR 4-4-0s, often

of the 'Intermediate' class, the forerunners of the 'Glens'.

The virtually hourly trains to Glasgow, which were mostly of six-bogie formation if they originated in Edinburgh, but heavier if they were running through, or carried through coaches, from the south, had a great variety of motive power: In common use were 'Scott' or, less often, 'Glen' 4-4-0s from the North British; 'Directors' of Great Central ancestry; and the new LNER 'Shires'. And, for so long as they lasted, there were occasional North British 'Atlantics'. Gresley 'Pacifics' were not unknown on Glasgow trains either. The two latter types were in the Aberdeen and Newcastle links respectively and were rostered for certain Glasgow trains to fill in time during which they would have otherwise been idle. Trains over the steep 50-mile road to Perth were usually worked by 'Scotts' or 'Glens'.

Between Edinburgh and Aberdeen, 'Pacifics' became increasingly common during the 1930s, though there was always the possibility of seeing an NBR 'Atlantic' or a 'Director' or 'Shire' 4-4-0, followed by its small pilot. Once, but only once, I saw a relief to an express from Aberdeen arriving at Waverley behind one of the ex-Great Eastern Railway inside-cylindered 4-6-0s of the '1500' class. This was one of the batch sent to work over the lines of the former Great North of Scotland Railway. At the time I saw it, this GER loco was of course an Aberdeen engine, and as such deserving of comment in that on the Edinburgh–Aberdeen service locos were usually changed at Dundee; Haymarket engines operating south of the latter city, and those shedded at Dundee, working from there to Aberdeen. Since the entire distance by rail from Edinburgh to Aberdeen was only about 130 miles, this rostering always seemed to me to be a very uneconomic procedure. No doubt the practice originated in NBR days, but in view of the increasing tendency in the 1930s for long through workings elsewhere on the LNER it

LNER Class A1, later A3, 'Pacific' No 2575 Galopin. This engine, which was built at Doncaster in 1924, was very familiar to the author in Edinburgh during the years 1933–37. Allowing for a certain flexibility in spelling, what more suitable name could be given to a Gresley 'Pacific'? Galopin, like all but four (later five) of the non-streamlined 'Pacifics', was named after a racehorse. Let us hope that the latter galloped to the benefit of the punters as satisfactorily as the loco did for the passengers!

Historical Model Railway Society ACW018

LNER Class D49 3-cylinder 4-4-0 No 264 Stirlingshire. The loco immediately behind the 'Shire' is the Class J39 0-6-0. These two classes were fitted with similar boilers.

Historical Model Railway Society ABT031

LNER 'Mikado' No 2001 was built in 1934 by Sir Nigel Gresley for heavy passenger service on the difficult Edinburgh–Aberdeen road. Although five more of the type were built, and all proved to be eminently capable of the work for which they were designed, for some reason, never satisfactorily explained to the author, these fine machines were vandalised during the World War Two by being rebuilt as ugly and not particularly efficient 'Pacifics'. Note the rotary cam poppet valve gear which was later replaced by Gresley's standard conjugated arrangement of the Walschaerts Gear, which was fitted from the start on the other five P2 class 2-8-2s, Nos 2002–6.

Historical Model Railway Society ABX234

seems strange that the custom was perpetuated. Even after the large Class P2 2-8-2s *Cock o' the North*, *Wolf of Badenoch* and the others came into regular service, engines continued normally to be changed at Dundee.

Over the Waverley route, from Edinburgh to Carlisle via Galashiels and Hawick, the heavy expresses, some of which continued south to Leeds and London over the Carlisle and Settle line of the former Midland Railway, were almost always hauled by 'Pacifics' or piloted NBR 'Atlantics'. I never saw a 'Shire' or a 'Director' on one of those workings.

When the P2s appeared, it was announced that they were to be used on the Carlisle as well as the Aberdeen road. To my knowledge this was never done, although the timetables in force over the two routes would have permitted such workings without difficulty.

The great 2-8-2s were lovely machines. I first saw the prototype, No 2001, standing in Stonehaven station in her early days on an Edinburgh–Aberdeen train, when for test purposes she (or he? – after all, the name was *Cock o' the North*) was working right through between the two terminal stations. Later, when the engine was in regular service, I often saw it moving through Princes Street Gardens, either at the head of a train, or coming or going from or to the shed. The soft exhaust (which, however, still plainly indicated that this was a three-cylinder engine) and the smoothly

P2 class 2-8-2 No 2001 Cock o' the North *leaving Waverley and passing through Princes Street gardens in Edinburgh, as described opposite.*

W Hermiston, The Transport Treasury

turning driving rod of the poppet valve gear combined to give an impression of effortless and almost silent power, quite the reverse of what had impressed me when watching a 'Woolwich' leave Mullingar, but nevertheless creating an image which has remained equally strongly in my mind.

While on the subject of three-cylinder engines, I will never forget the unique sound of a Gresley loco starting a heavy train; or an even more vivid memory, running at about 20 miles per hour through the cutting between Waverley station and the Haymarket tunnel. The high tensile steel connecting and coupling rods, combined with the often slightly 'off beat' exhaust (do I need to remind readers of the negative side of the conjugated valve gear?) produced a signature tune resembling that of no other type of British locomotive.

I understand that after World War Two, when KJ Cooke, a Great Western man, was Chief Mechanical Engineer of the Eastern and North Eastern regions of British Railways, he introduced a 'high tech' optical system of aligning valve motions and connecting rods which resulted in a considerable tightening up and did away with the 'Gresley ring'. No doubt the engines were the better for this treatment, but one wonders whether, if the ghost of Gresley had been hovering over Doncaster in those later days, he might have said, as OV Bulleid is related to have done when someone at Inchicore played him a record of a rebuilt 'Merchant Navy' 'Pacific' starting from Waterloo – "These are not my engines."

As well as the mainline trains from Edinburgh to Newcastle, Aberdeen, Glasgow, Perth and Carlisle, there were a number of others. Of such trains I remember the stopping trains to Dundee on both the main and Fife coast lines; those to Stirling via the Forth Bridge and Alloa; the North Berwick services which started their journeys on the East Coast Main Line and the 'locals' to Hawick on the Waverley route. I also remember the trains which went no further than Galashiels on that line, but did so by a circuitous path via Peebles.

In addition to the avowedly suburban trains, there was a secondary service to Glasgow. This service *did not* proceed to Queen Street High Level station in that city via Linlithgow and Falkirk as the expresses did, but operated with many stops through the central coalfield area of Scotland via Bathgate, to Queen Street Low Level, and thence

onwards to the Glasgow suburban terminus of Hyndland. A feature of this service was that since in the Glasgow area it was a suburban working, the engines carried the destination board 'Hyndland' on their smokeboxes when leaving Edinburgh. These boards were red with white lettering.

As regards the engines on the secondary services, various types of North British 4-4-0 operated to Dundee over both routes, to Hyndland, to Galashiels and to Berwick. 'Directors' and 'Shires' ran to Dundee, though I never saw one of the latter type on the coastal route. The services to Stirling and to North Berwick were interesting in that they relied for the most part on Gresley Vls, three-cylinder 2-6-2Ts, most serviceable machines, which, however, are largely forgotten now. The two suburban services which I best remember were that on the circular line, and the one to North

LNER Class N2 0-6-2T No 894 heading a Glasgow–Edinburgh stopping train emerging from the North Queensferry tunnel. The destination board is of the old North British pattern with white lettering on a red ground. N2s were not often seen in Edinburgh, and then, in the author's experience, only when working trains to and from Glasgow over the Bathgate route. The design of the N2s dated from 1921; they were originally introduced on the Great Northern Railway for London suburban traffic, but many were built after the Grouping, some specifically for service in Scotland.

Historical Model Railway Society ADG404

LNER V1 class 2-6-2T No 2917. The leading vehicle of the train is an ex-North British coach. The end of the two-to-one combination lever, for actuating the middle piston valve, is visible at the front of the valve chest of the right cylinder of the loco. These engines worked Edinburgh suburban trains and stopping trains to Stirling and North Berwick during the author's Scottish years. However, the last occasion on which he travelled behind one was on a journey between Newcastle Central station and Tyne Commission Quay in 1962. Historical Model Railway Society AAL502

Leith. Trains on the former, anything from three to six bogies, were commonly hauled by engines of the second series of North British inside-cylindered 4-4-2Ts, though V1s also appeared.

The North Leith services had no engines at all in the conventional sense, as they were operated by steam railcars. These vehicles were painted green and white, as were some of the centre corridor coaches for excursion work which started to appear from Doncaster in the 1930s. While this colour scheme may have been suitable for conventional coaches, it was not a success for steam railcars – smoke soon reduced the white to a shabby grey. The tunnels on the North Leith branch did not help either.

Waverley station, with its 19 platforms, usually had three pilots at work: two at the west end and one at the east. These were standard North British 0-6-0Ts dating from around the turn of the century. The intermittent sound of their loud exhausts, interspersed with the panting of their air pumps when at rest (the NBR, like the Caledonian, used the Westinghouse brake) has remained in my memory as one of the features of Waverley. So often, during my four years in Scotland, did I see these little engines that even now, at least 65 years later, I remember the numbers of the two which normally worked the west end of the station: Nos 9826 and 9828, formerly NBR Nos 826 and 828.

Goods trains were not as frequently seen as passenger ones, except when actually travelling, but fortunately I did a fair amount of getting around by rail and got to know the Aberdeen and Glasgow main lines quite well. Much of the district between Edinburgh and Glasgow was a colliery area, and the same was true of a considerable part of the county of Fife between Edinburgh and Dundee. In those areas one saw the three varieties of North British 0-6-0 which I always considered to be roughly comparable to the SG3s, SGs, and QGs of the GNR(I). Other 0-6-0s were the post-Grouping J38s, a Gresley design with 4'7" wheels and with the same relatively large boiler that was used on the 'Shire' and 'Hunt' 4-4-0s. Apart from their smaller wheels, these six-coupled engines were similar to the better known J39s which were more of a 'mixed traffic' than a purely goods type. I have heard that the design of the entire class (J38 and J39) was a development of the standard large 0-6-0s of the erstwhile North Eastern Railway. Am I right in thinking that the J38 and J39 was the only new post-1922 Gresley design which did not incorporate three cylinders? Despite their unglamorous appearance I will always

remember the J39s, since the last LNER locomotive which I saw in steam, other than in preservation, was one of the class (at Carlisle in about 1965). The last two types of LNER engine behind which I travelled, also in the 1960s, were a V1 tank and one of the just mentioned old North Eastern 0-6-0s. The trains concerned were the Norwegian boat connections between Newcastle Central station and Tyne Commission Quay, North Shields.

There were larger London and North Eastern goods engines than 0-6-0s at work in Scotland. It was rare to make a journey of any length from Edinburgh on the Glasgow or Aberdeen roads without seeing one of the ex-GCR 2-8-0s – as widely used for mineral and heavy freight engines as were their 'Director' cousins for passenger work. Gresley had a high regard for Robinson's engines, and for

LNER Class J37 (ex-NBR 'S' class 'heavy goods') 0-6-0 No 9454 (NBR No 454). These big engines, with 19½" x 26" cylinders, were the most powerful goods locos to work on the North British lines until the coming of the Robinson 2-8-0s after the Grouping. There were 104 in the class, all built between 1914 and 1921, some with the Westinghouse brake, making them suitable for passenger work, and the rest with engine steam brake only. In 1921, some very interesting trials took place between one of these locos, a Great Western '28xx' 2-8-0 and a North Eastern 'T3' 3-cylinder 0-8-0. The latter engine just about wiped the floor with the Great Western engine. Whether, but for the Grouping, the North British, as a result of these trials, might have produced some 0-8-0s of its own is an interesting speculation

Historical Model Railway Society ACC717

LNER J39 0-6-0 No 1505. These engines, which had 5'2" driving wheels, were suitable for use on excursion and other moderately-timed passenger trains, as well as general goods work. A virtually identical class of 0-6-0, the J38s, which worked mainly in Scotland, was distinguishable from the J39 only by smaller wheels (4'8") and the absence of the vestigial splashers of the latter machines.

Historical Model Railway Society ACW103

LNER Robinson O4 class 2-8-0 No 6534. In the later 1920s and the 1930s, there were a number of these Great Central mineral engines on the ex-NBR lines. These justly famed machines provided much appreciated power for the heavy coal-trains between the Fife and Lothian coalfields and the ports. Note the provision of 'back sand'. Much of the work on colliery sidings and nearby lines involved tender-first running.

Historical Model Railway Society AAK015

Robinson himself, and had a number of 'Directors' specifically built for work in Scotland, an action which was paralleled by the building of new Robinson 4-6-2Ts for work in the north-east of England. Ironically perhaps, in view of the distaste (to use no stronger word) which Gresley's successor Edward Thompson showed for all of Gresley's standard designs, it was the ex-Great Central Railway medium-sized 0-6-0, the 'Pom Pom', which Thompson included in a list of engines for future production as standard types, along with his own designs.

Other freight engines remembered are the K2 two-cylinder 2-6-0s, some of which were given names and side windows to their rather spartan (Stirling/Ivatt) cabs and sent to work on the West Highland line. These 'Moguls' occasionally got to Edinburgh on fitted goods workings. The dock lines at Leith, Edinburgh's port, could usually be relied on to produce a couple of the small outside-cylindered 0-6-0T shunters, whilst the diminutive 0-4-0ST 'pugs', with their dumb buffers, were always in evidence there. Express fish trains from Aberdeen were much in evidence, their locos commonly being 'Pacifics' or, after about 1935, V2 2-6-2s ('Green Arrows').

Before commenting on the passenger vehicles seen in the Edinburgh area of the LNER, I should mention four locomotive types which one was certain to see on journeys to Glasgow or Aberdeen, but only one of which I ever saw in Edinburgh. There were, first in Glasgow, the N2 0-6-2Ts, the first of which had been designed by Gresley for suburban service on the former Great Northern Railway, but whose Scottish examples had been built after the Grouping specifically for Glasgow suburban service. On a very few occasions I saw one of these on an Edinburgh–Glasgow Queen Street Low Level–Hyndland stopping train. Also seen in Glasgow were ex-North British 0-6-2Ts, which banked passenger trains up the heavy gradient from Queen Street High

Level to Cowlairs, a duty formerly carried out by a winding engine and a cable. The third type of engine not seen in Edinburgh was the standard small 4-4-0 of the Great North of Scotland Railway, examples of which were always in evidence at Aberdeen. These were distinctive-looking machines with high driving wheels, rather low-pitched boilers and large side-window cabs with a sort of clerestory arrangement on their roofs. An extra touch of individuality was given by their being numbered in the 6800 series, immediately after the GCR locomotives. The fourth locomotive type was the 0-4-2 shunting tank, also of the GNSR. There were two subtypes of this design, both of which survived until at least the 1950s. I saw one on the Aberdeen dock lines as late as 1957.

The 1930s were as interesting a period for coaches as for locomotives. When I went to Edinburgh in 1933, North British vehicles were common – they were still being used on the express services between Edinburgh and Glasgow and Edinburgh and Perth, and also appeared in some Edinburgh–Carlisle trains. These straight-forward looking, wooden side-corridor bogies were comfortable enough, but had few frills in the third class. From the passenger point of view, the thirds were about equal in comfort to the contemporary wooden mainline stock being turned out by Inchicore. However, they looked a little less austere internally, thanks to some lincrusta linings in areas where the GSR coaches had match-boarding.

Even by 1933–34 not all Edinburgh–Glasgow expresses were made up of ex-North British vehicles. For example, the Leeds–Glasgow 'Diner' was composed of modern bow-ended stock with buckeye couplings; and the London–Glasgow 'Queen of Scots' all-Pullman train was also a thoroughly up to date train, including its couplings. There were no restrictions on mixing modern LNER and older NBR (or NER) vehicles in the same train, in

LNER 3-cylinder mixed traffic 2-6-2 No 4835, of Class V2, heading a fast goods. These capable locos were often seen on fish trains ex-Aberdeen on the former NBR northern main line, as well as on passenger and goods workings over much of the LNER system. Writing in LNER Steam, *0S Nock stated that the V2s (the 'Green Arrows') were frequently timed at 90 mph or slightly higher on both the East Coast and Great Central main lines.*

Historical Model Railway Society ACW113

contrast to the situation with the BUT railcars and trailers on the GNR(I) in 1957. For example, the down 10.00 ex-King's Cross (the 'Flying Scotsman'), or its 10.05 relief in summer, conveyed through vehicles for Glasgow, Perth and Aberdeen as well as those which went only to Edinburgh. The Glasgow and Perth through coaches, modern London and North Eastern stock, would be taken forward from Edinburgh at the heads of trains of ex-NBR carriages.

Mention of through coaches on the 'Scotsman' reminds me that, except during the darkest part of the winter, the period between about 17.40 and 18.10 provided perhaps the maximum amount of interest at the west end of Waverley station. As soon as the 'Scotsman' or its relief arrived at the down main platform, which served the long through line on the south side of the station, the 'Pacific' at its head came off and hurried away to Haymarket

shed. Then the engine of the Perth train, normally a 'Scott' or 'Glen' 4-4-0, which had been standing at the head of its train in one of the bay platforms, would come forward and set back against the Perth through brake composite coach at the head of the London train, and then take this away to the front of its own train in the bay. The above procedure would be repeated by the loco of the Glasgow train (probably a 'Shire' or a 'Director') which would have been waiting in another of the west-facing bays. In this case, however, there would be two or three vehicles from London to Glasgow, rather than a single coach. Finally the Aberdeen engine, a North British 'Atlantic' or, more commonly from 1935 onwards, a 'Pacific', would back down on to the head of the Aberdeen portion of the 'Scotsman'. While the above proceedings were taking place, the east end pilot would have lifted the last couple of coaches and the triplet restaurant car set from the back end of the 'Scotsman', and replaced them with a fresh dining car and a couple of tail vehicles. Then the exodus would start: first the Aberdeen, then the Glasgow and finally the Perth.

Once, when watching this nightly exodus, I saw what could have been a nasty sideways collision. The Aberdeen and the Glasgow trains, standing on adjoining but converging tracks, each started at the same time. Presumably one of the drivers mistook or ignored a signal, but whatever the reason the two engines, an 'Atlantic' on the Aberdeen train and a 'Director' on the Glasgow, started to move forward together to the accompaniment of the usual loud exhausts and clouds of steam from the cylinder cocks, each making for the V at the apex of the converging tracks. Almost immediately there was a flurry of activity – porters, shunters and various others materialised from where they had hitherto been concealed, and with shouts and upraised arms succeeded in stopping the Aberdeen train before any harm was done.

Mention of a 'Director' 4-4-0 reminds me that whilst on their parent Great Central Railway, some of these big inside-cylindered machines were named after directors of the company: *Butler Henderson* for example. The post-Grouping engines built for service in Scotland carried on the tradition of the NBR 'Scott' class in using the names of characters from the novels of Sir Walter Scott. Hence, in place of the names of worthy, but undeniably English, bygone Great Central directors, one saw such sonorous and thoroughly Scottish appellations as *Laird of Balmawhapple* and *Luckie Mucklebackit*. Maybe it was as well that none of the Scottish 'Directors' ever served with the Great Central: *Maid of Lorne* or *Haystoun of Bucklaw* might have seemed a bit incongruous at the head of a Leicester–Nottingham stopping train in the flat and placid English Midlands.

Returning to coaching stock, as well as ex-

North British and standard East Coast vehicles on mainline trains, one occasionally saw old NER bow-ended carriages. These were very similar in contour to the East Coast standard coaches, but with conventional screw couplings and concertina corridor gangways. On the suburban trains, where one saw ex-NER as well as NBR coaches, there was an increasing use of new semi-corridor non-gangwayed vehicles built to Gresley's (Bulleid's) design since the Grouping.

There were three types of catering vehicle in general use on the Scottish section of the LNER during the 1930s. First, there was the standard East Coast design, which could be divided into three sub-types: single restaurant cars, the older ones with centre kitchens, the newer with kitchen accommodation at one end; second, triplet articulated sets, used only on Anglo-Scottish through services; and finally the recently introduced buffet cars, whose accommodation comprised seating, a bar and a small kitchen. (I once made an error of phraseology when travelling in one of these latter cars: after my time in Scotland travelling between Carlisle and Newcastle-on-Tyne, and reflecting my GNR(I) experience, I asked for a plain tea. What I received was just a cup of tea.)

Next among LNER Scottish catering vehicles were the Pullman cars. Aside from the all-Pullman 'Queen of Scots', some trains between Edinburgh and Glasgow and Edinburgh and Carlisle included a Pullman in their make-up. My recollection is that, contrary to the state of affairs after the Pullmans were first introduced on the GSR in Ireland, persons requiring meals were not charged any supplementary fee over and above the cost of the food and/or drink ordered. On the other hand, supplementary fares were certainly charged on the 'Queen of Scots' on which I once travelled from Edinburgh to Glasgow. For the record, the train was composed of eight bogies, and the engine from Edinburgh onwards was a 'Director'.

Finally, as regards LNER catering vehicles in use in the 1930s, there were some elderly clerestory-roofed cars which had originated on the Midland Railway. These had presumably come to the LNER after the Grouping, and must have been supplied by the Midland before 1923 to provide a meal service in the through trains between London (St Pancras), Leeds and Edinburgh. In the 1930s at least one train each way between Edinburgh and Carlisle included one of these cars in its composition. I once travelled in one of these old Midland relics, but on a line about as far removed from central England as can be imagined – the West Highland, from Glasgow to Fort William. However, at the head of the train concerned, in the summer of 1934, there were two 4-4-0s, which was thoroughly in keeping with Midland practice for heavy trains and/or steep gradients. Presumably the old dining car felt that all had not changed utterly. As a matter of interest, two or three days after this journey I moved on from Fort William to Mallaig, over the West Highland extension line, with its many curves and 1:50 gradients. The train engine was a J37, the largest type of North British 0-6-0, a Scottish 'Big D'.

So much for the types of catering vehicle which one might have encountered in a journey from or to Edinburgh in the 1930s. There was, however, one other sort which I never saw in motion, but two members of which stood in a siding at the south-west end of Waverley station for several years. This type comprised two massive 12-wheeled, all-steel restaurant cars which had been constructed by Cravens for the North British in 1919. One was a centre kitchen vehicle, whilst the other had the cooking facilities at one end. Each of these vehicles weighed not far short of 50 tons, so it is not surprising that although they had been repainted in London and North Eastern colours, they remained unused for the whole of my time in Edinburgh. To what extent they had

been used in pre-Grouping days, I do not know, but they certainly represented a bad investment by the NBR. In practical terms these heavy diners were of little more use than the old horse-drawn 'Dandy coach' which once operated the short branch between Drumburgh Junction and Port Carlisle, but which for many years after its withdrawal from service stood, as a relic of the past, on a raised mounting on the north side of the Waverley station.

The Drumburgh to Port Carlisle branch line of the North British was no more in Scotland than was the line from which it diverged, the Carlisle–Silloth section of the premier Scottish railway. However, despite the fact that in pre-Grouping days the North Eastern provided the locomotives for the expresses over the North British between Berwick and Edinburgh, the Scottish company was no stranger to English soil. The lines just mentioned, plus the English section of the Hexham to Riccarton Junction connection, and the Rothbury–Morpeth and Scotsgap and Redesmouth branches, all combined to provide quite a tidy English mileage for the North British. In the terms of services operated, the mileage was augmented by the Scottish company's running powers over the North Eastern between Hexham and Newcastle. These running powers gave rise to the somewhat unexpected sight that I encountered the first time I alighted from a southbound (ex-Edinburgh) train at Newcastle. Facing me in a bay platform as I approached the station exit, and in a position from which it appeared to be facing Edinburgh, was a North British 4-4-0, having just arrived with a train. The situation may be summarised by saying that English locos came into Newcastle from Scotland, whilst Scottish locos came into the same station from England.

While on the subject of Riccarton Junction, the late GB Howden, General Manager and previously Chief Engineer of the GNR(I), who was an ex-North British man, told me that during the General Strike in Britain in 1926 he was sent to Riccarton to act as a signalman. That railway outpost was a sort of 'super' Inny Junction (for Cavan), important in itself but miles from anywhere and consisting merely of the junction station, other necessary installations and some railwaymen's houses in the middle of the wild upland English–Scottish border country. GBH recounted how, at the height of the strike, he was marooned in his cabin, to which the local railwaymen laid siege by attacking it with lumps of coal!

We have just been talking of restaurant cars and running powers. These two subjects bring me to the last specifically London and North Eastern recollection of my days in Scotland. Shortly before Christmas 1935, our entire family had occasion to travel from Edinburgh to Southampton. Almost certainly, the route offering the shortest time would have been by direct train to London (King's Cross), across

London and onwards to Southampton by Southern Railway from Waterloo. However, I knew a more interesting way. There was a daily through carriage from Glasgow to Southampton Docks, presumably for the benefit of travellers proceeding to France or the Channel Islands by the SR night steamers. This coach left Glasgow shortly before 09.00 on the Edinburgh train which also conveyed the through coaches attached to the 10.00 up 'Scotsman' (or its relief in summer). At York the coach left the East Coast Main Line and travelled to Sheffield, from where it continued by courtesy of the ex-GCR to Banbury. There it moved on to Great Western metals, over which it ran, via Oxford and Reading, to Basingstoke on the former LSWR main line, and so finished its journey to Southampton over the Southern Railway. Although this long-distance vehicle did not leave the East Coast line until it got to York, it was detached from the London train at Newcastle, where it became part of the Newcastle–Cardiff through train which was

LMS 'Pacific' No 6204 Princess Louise *at Princes Street station, Edinburgh, in 1935. Note the very typical late nineteenth-/early twentieth-century signal gantry. No 6204 could have been a Polmadie (Glasgow) engine. I rather doubt if any 'Pacifics' were stationed at Dalry Road (Edinburgh) shed in the mid 1930s.*

HN Shepherd, The Transport Treasury

operated as a joint LNER/GWR enterprise. Trains from each company provided the service on alternate days; on the day on which we travelled it was the turn of the LNER to operate southwards. I remember having lunch in the first class end of a standard centre-kitchen Doncaster-built diner. This has remained in my memory for two reasons: first, because although the family was, as always, travelling third class, we were given seats in the first class section due to the heavy pre-Christmas traffic; and second, because the green leather upholstery was sufficiently unusual to have left a permanent impression. Despite the relatively luxurious and unaccustomed surroundings in which we consumed our lunch, I experienced a slight feeling of disappointment. At that time I had had virtually no contact with the Great Western, though I was fairly well-travelled on the other three British railway groups. I had hoped that our through carriage might be attached to a GWR train, and that we might sample the attractions of a Western diner as new experiences.

In the event there was heavy fog, and we arrived very late in Southampton. Nevertheless, the trip was interesting and provided me with my only journey over the Great Central main line north of High Wycombe. I do not remember what type of locomotive we had between Newcastle and Sheffield, but south of the latter city the LNER provided a 'Sandringham' 4-6-0. Darkness and fog prevented identification of the Western and Southern engines.

So much for the pre-war LNER in Scotland. The LMS also served Edinburgh, but neither the number of services nor the variety of locomotives and rolling stock were equal to what were to be seen on the ex-NBR lines. For a start, the seven platforms at Princes Street terminus were 'small beer' compared to the 17, plus two suburban, of the Waverley. And secondly, passenger services were confined to

Glasgow, Carlisle and the south; Stirling, Perth and Aberdeen by courtesy of the LNER as far as Falkirk; and the three suburban routes, to Balerno, Barnton and Leith.

Paradoxically, it was these latter services, and particularly the one to Balerno, some six or seven miles from Princes Street on a branch which formed a loop off the main line to Glasgow and Carlisle, which provided the greatest interest. The branch had many severe curves which necessitated the use of specially built four-wheeled coaching stock. This stock was no miscellaneous collection of old nineteenth century vehicles spinning out their last days – the coaches had been built since World War One and were constructed to the full limits of the loading gauge. Balerno carriages sometimes appeared on Barnton and Leith trains, but generally the latter were made up of a mixture of modern LMS and older ex-Caledonian non-corridor compartment bogies.

Engines on all three suburban passenger services were invariably ex-Caledonian tanks. These were of two classes: the older and smaller were a Drummond design (Drummond had earlier produced something similar for the North British and was later to build much larger examples of the type, the 'M7s', for the LSWR). The larger Caledonian engines were a development by MacIntosh of Drummond's machines. I understand that the later engines, although more powerful than the pioneers, which had the nickname of 'threepenny bits', were not so popular with enginemen, the reason being that their larger tanks did not give so good a view of the edges of platforms. The drawback for a suburban engine making many stops is obvious.

Both the LMS and LNER ran approximately hourly express services between Edinburgh and Glasgow. The times of the LMS trains, operating over the more heavily graded line, were not quite equal to the best that the London and North Eastern could produce. However, neither concern was able to provide a really fast

An ex-Caledonian Railway 0-4-4T No 55166 on a local train at Balerno Junction in February 1952. This engine has not yet been disfigured (in the author's opinion) by the replacement of its Drummond chimney by one of the 'stovepipes' imposed on members of its class in their last years. In view of the fact that Drummond's renowned T9 4-4-0s of the London and South Western/Southern Railways, which had a similar type of chimney, were also given 'stovepipes' in their declining years, one wonders if the Drummond design was less than fully efficient as a draught producer.

J Robertson, The Transport Treasury

service over the approximately 45 miles between the two cities, as there were several speed restrictions due to the colliery workings on each line. So far as I remember, the best non-stop time was 55 minutes by the LNER. Most trains on either route, however, made at least two stops. The LMS did not have a second route to Glasgow corresponding to the ex-North British line through Bathgate to Queen Street Low Level and Hyndland, but it did run so-called 'Glasgow locals' as well as expresses.

These LMS Glasgow expresses were almost invariably six-bogie formations, including a Pullman restaurant car, a type of vehicle fairly widely used on the ex-Caledonian lines in the mid-1930s. The most usual locomotives were the large 'Dunalastairs' (ex-Caledonian 4-4-0s), though Midland 'Compound' 4-4-0s were also used. Engine power on the 'locals' was generally similar to that on the expresses.

Edinburgh shed (Dalry Road) did not seem to have any other type of locomotive, other than the two mentioned, for the Glasgow trains, but Glasgow occasionally produced some variety to break the monotony of the 4-4-0s. Among types sometimes seen were inside- and outside-cylindered 4-6-0s and 4-6-2Ts, in each case former Caledonian machines. One saw 'Crab' 'Moguls', with their steeply inclined outside cylinders, but in my experience these were mainly on trains to Carstairs and southwards to Carlisle, rather than to Glasgow.

Most of these latter services worked through to London, Manchester or Liverpool, sometimes as complete trains, but more often as Edinburgh through coaches, combined with Glasgow portions at Carstairs, a practice which could produce some interesting exercises in marshalling. For example, a train might leave Edinburgh with sections for both

Manchester and Liverpool, and would meet another similar formation from Glasgow at Carstairs. The two would then be split up and remarshalled, with both Manchester portions at the front and the two Liverpool sets at the rear, these to be detached at Preston. The 'Baby Scot' or other large 4-6-0 which had brought the Glasgow train to Carstairs would usually work right through to Manchester. In the later 1930s 'Jubilees' and 'Black Fives' became increasingly common on these duties.

On Edinburgh/Glasgow to Manchester/Liverpool services, catering facilities were usually provided between Glasgow and Manchester by standard LMS dining cars. A number of such vehicles, with end kitchens and mounted on six-wheeled bogies, came into service in the 1930s, supplanting the old London and North Western cars (West Coast Joint Stock?), also 12-wheelers. Some of these, however, were still in evidence up to 1935. I remember seeing one of them, with its Pullman-type vestibules, on a separate Edinburgh relief to the 10.00 ex-Euston (the 'Royal Scot'). I first made the acquaintance of these cars in the early 1920s when, on annual visits to grandparents in the south of England, we saw and sometimes used them on the 'Irish Mail' between Holyhead and London. Probably the last time I saw one, and certainly the last time I was ever in one, was in 1935, travelling over the Kyle of Lochalsh branch of the former Highland railway.

Returning to catering facilities between Edinburgh and Manchester/Liverpool, during the Christmas holiday period of 1934 our entire family travelled from Edinburgh to Liverpool, preparatory to embarking on a cruise. (The journey to Southampton made at the same time a year later was undertaken for the same purpose.) At this busy time of year it was necessary to duplicate the normal train, with the result that there was no dining car on the Liverpool portion. However, the LMS rose to the occasion by providing luncheon baskets.

The guard canvassed the train for orders for baskets at Carstairs, and these appeared at Carlisle.

In nineteenth and early twentieth century days, the luncheon/ breakfast/dinner basket was a standard feature of long-distance railway travel and was advertised in public timetable booklets. Just what might have been available from a Caledonian/London and North Western basket before 1914 I do not know, but on the Midland Great Western (of Ireland) at that time one could, for three shillings (15p), be supplied with a luncheon basket containing half a chicken, with ham or tongue, bread, cheese and butter and either a half bottle of claret, two glasses of sherry or a bottle of ale or stout. Correspondingly well filled breakfast baskets were available on the MGWR, but in their case the charge was only half a crown (12½p). These baskets could be obtained at Dublin, Mullingar, Athlone, Claremorris, Cavan and Sligo; so, provided one had the appropriate amount of money, there was no excuse for going hungry on the Midland. Except, apparently, if one joined a train at Galway, in which case it would seem that one tightened one's belt and waited until the train got to Athlone.

Petty pilfering was obviously as common in the second decade of the twentieth century as it is at the present, for in the supplementary appendix to the GNR(I) working timetable of 1915 it was laid down that guards were responsible for ensuring that all the fixtures (knives, forks, spoons etc, and not forgetting the corkscrews) of baskets were returned to the catering department at the end of each journey. As a matter of interest, the same appendix instructed guards to inspect the toilet compartments (termed 'lavatories' in those days) several times on each Dublin–Belfast or Belfast–Derry journey, and to replace soiled with clean towels as necessary.

I can remember neither the contents of, nor the charge for, an LMS luncheon basket in

December 1934, but since at that time a four course lunch at the prestigious Royal Hibernian Hotel in Dublin cost three shillings and sixpence (17½p) and a three course one (admittedly with somewhat scanty servings) could be obtained in at least one establishment in Edinburgh for one shilling and sixpence (7½p), the LMS charge is unlikely to have been much greater than the Midland Great Western's price of 20 years earlier.

I have mentioned using an ex-London and North Western dining car on the former Highland Railway. The trip involved was the first section of an interesting summer day's journey from Achnashellach, on the Kyle line, to Edinburgh. From the late 1930s until the end of steam, the Dingwall–Kyle of Lochalsh road was worked largely by 'Black Five' 4-6-0s, but when I travelled over it in 1935 the ex-Highland 'Clan Goods' were still strongly in evidence, and it was behind one of these locomotives that I journeyed to Inverness. The 'Clan Goods' were 4-6-0s with 20½"x 26" cylinders and 5'3" wheels. Four were built in 1918 and four more the following year. In general appearance they had a close resemblance to the better known mainline passenger 'Clan' 4-6-0s, and like these, and also the 'Claughtons' of the London and North Western, had their outside motion partly obscured by valances. Despite Maunsell's 2-6-0s, the first of which appeared in 1915, it was obviously considered slightly indecent for locomotives to expose their working parts. It is tempting to ascribe this to Scottish puritanism, but then one remembers Urie's big 4-6-0s of 1918, and although an LSWR man, Urie was impeccably Scottish. However, his predecessor and mentor on the LSWR, Dugald Drummond, had used valances, so perhaps Urie was untypical in designing locomotives that were, as regards their Walschaert's valve gear, outright 'flashers'.

Here we must flit back very briefly to my second favourite Midland Great Western. Is it generally known that Robert Urie, of the London and South Western Railway, had a son who became Assistant Mechanical Engineer at Broadstone under WH Morton? Urie Junior, subsequently returned to his ancestral Scotland to become the last CME of the Highland, and later Mechanical Engineer (Scotland) in LMS days.

As interesting as the 'Clan Goods' were, there were two other ex-Highland engines seen on that summer day, 67 years ago, which intrigued me more than the Kyle branch 4-6-0s. The first of these, seen at Dingwall, was one of the last batch of 'Loch' 4-4-0s, Loch Ashie. Although this engine was built in 1917, it was in all principal respects identical to the original David Jones machines of 1896, and had the distinctive external features associated with that engineer's locomotives, including the louvred chimney and the slightly domed cab. To digress for a moment on to the subject of cabs, it has always seemed to me remarkable that, in view of the very harsh winter conditions experienced on the Highland, neither Jones, Peter Drummond, Smith nor Cumming (who succeeded Jones in that order) provided their engines with side-window cabs, even though this refinement was to be found on the Great North of Scotland Railway, with which the Highland was in daily contact. Side-window cabs were also to be seen on all of the more recent types of North British engines which the Highland encountered at Perth.

A total of 18 'Lochs' were built between 1896 and 1917, so it was not altogether surprising that I should meet one of them during almost a whole day's travelling on the Highland in the mid-1930s. The other loco seen for the first time that day, this time at Aviemore, was a much rarer bird. This machine was Snaigow, ex-Highland No 75, one of two large outside-cylindered 4-4-0s built by Christopher Cumming in 1917. In general appearance Snaigow and her sister, Durn, looked like shortened 'Clans'; or perhaps it

One of the heavy goods 4-6-0s of the former Highland Railway which were designed by Christopher Cumming (or his chief draughtsman), and built by Hawthorn, Leslie in 1918–19. Despite the close resemblance of these 'Clan Goods', as they were sometimes called, to the better known 'Clan' 4-6-0 passenger engines, there were some differences between the two classes, the most obvious to a superficial observer being the absence of the vestigial driving wheel splashers of the 'Clans' on the passenger engines. The location of this picture is probably Inverness, but the date has not been established. Note how someone, possibly a cleaner, has bestowed temporary 'Clan' status on this grimy old workhorse.

W Hermiston, The Transport Treasury

would be more accurate to say that the 'Clans' resembled elongated editions of the 4-4-0s, as the latter engines predated the former by two years. The principal dimensions of *Snaigow* and *Durn* were: cylinders 21" x 26", boiler pressure 170 lbs psi, and coupled wheels 6'0" diameter.

I do not remember seeing either a 'Clan' or a 'Castle' during this, my first, journey over the Highland, and indeed the only clear memories I have of either of these types of 4-6-0 are from the ex-Caledonian line to Oban, to which several were transferred after Stanier 'Black Fives' became available for service on the Highland lines. Two of this latter class headed the train from Inverness to Perth in which I travelled in an ex-North British through

carriage from the former city to Edinburgh Waverley. Despite the fact that the LMS (ex-Caledonian) Railway ran through services from Edinburgh to Stirling, Perth and Aberdeen (over the LNER for most of the way to Stirling), the through service from Inverness to Edinburgh in 1935 remained, as it had been in pre-Grouping days, firmly in the hands of the North British (LNER) between Perth and Edinburgh. All through coaches were provided by that company over both the original route, via Forres, and the newer and shorter line, over Slochd summit. An extension of these North British/Highland services was the sleeping car connection between London (King's Cross) and Lossiemouth, a fishing port on the southern shore of the Moray Firth. Before

Here we see the ex-Highland Railway 4-4-0 No 73, Snaigow, *towards the end of its days as LMS No 14522. This engine, and its sister No 74,* Durn, *were built by Hawthorn, Leslie in 1917. It was the first completely new type of loco to be introduced by Christopher Cumming, who had come to the Highland from the North British two years earlier. Note the strong 'family' resemblance to the loco shown in the previous picture.*

JT Rutherford, The Transport Treasury

1923 it had been the Great North of Scotland Company, and not the Highland, which served Lossiemouth; so presumably when the sleeping car service was established, the vehicles travelled via the Speyside line of the GNS/LNER north of Aviemore, thus both commencing and finishing their journey on the London and North Eastern. There can hardly have been much terminus to terminus through traffic by that sleeping car service, so there must have been a reasonable amount of patronage from and to intermediate stations. Just when the service started, and whether it was in any way connected with the fact that Ramsay MacDonald, who was Prime Minister in 1924 and from 1929 to 1935, was a native of Lossiemouth, I do not know. This long-distance sleeping car service, from London to the north-east of Scotland, was paralleled by

another LNER sleeping car facility between King's Cross and Fort William. This latter service used the former North British West Highland line – no doubt the main reason for its existence was to cater for travellers to Skye and the outer islands using the shipping connections from Mallaig.

I have mentioned the ex-London and North Western diner on the Dingwall to Kyle of Lochalsh line, but there were also former North Western ordinary passenger coaches in use there, of the narrow-bodied variety, dating from the 1920s. Older Irish readers may remember that a few of this type, along with some examples of the larger sort of pre-1914 stock, were acquired as stopgaps by the GNR(I) about 1947.

Throughout the four years of my residence in Edinburgh, there was steady progress in the provision of up to date coaching stock for the Scottish services of both the LNER and the LMS. This was the period during which wide windows became standard for side-corridor compartment vehicles, together with three-a-side seating with armrests in third class compartments. The LMS was ahead of the rival company as regards the wide windows, whilst, in my experience at least, the LNER was to the fore with three-a-side seating.

However, during the second half of the 1930s, all new third class side-corridor coaches of each company had both wide windows and three-a-side seating. The LMS was definitely the first to introduce centre-corridor thirds for ordinary mainline service; indeed they started to do so as early as about 1930. 'Open' thirds built at that time were wooden bodied and had two side windows for each seating section, one of which was a traditional drop light. Many of the centre-corridor thirds built in the 1930s by the LNER were specifically designed for excursion work and were painted green and cream, as has been mentioned with reference to the colour scheme of the steam railcars. Most new first class side-corridor coaches had three-a-side seating, although the London and North Eastern built some two-a-side firsts for service in the 'Flying Scotsman' sets. The weight ratio of these latter vehicles worked out at about 1¼ tons per seat. At the other end of the scale the old 100-seat thirds of the GNR(I), which I have mentioned earlier, had a ratio of around a quarter ton per seat.

Why the LMS continued to turn out new coaches fitted with the traditional screw couplings and side buffers I do not know. In contrast, automatic couplings had been standard on Great Northern (England) and East Coast Joint Stock for many years, and were being fitted to all new LNER corridor vehicles built in the 1930s and had also appeared on the Great Western some years previously. Even the vehicles of the semi-streamlined LMS 'Coronation Scot' were joined together in the time-honoured manner.

Mention of a streamlined train reminds me that I saw little of the London and North Eastern's streamliners. The first of them, the 'Silver Jubilee', introduced in 1935, did not operate north of Newcastle, whilst the 'Coronation', which did serve Edinburgh, did not appear until 1937, the year in which I returned to Ireland. However, from 1935 onwards a streamlined A4 'Pacific', which was normally spare at Newcastle, quite often appeared at Waverley. I understand that the allocation of the first four streamlined 'Pacifics' – *Silver Jubilee, Silver Link, Silver King* and *Silver Fox* – was for two engines to be shedded at King's Cross and that one of these normally worked the 'Jubilee' trains, down in the evening and up in the early morning. A third engine was spare at Newcastle (Gateshead shed), and was prepared each morning in time to work the up streamline service in case of a late failure of the King's Cross engine. The fourth loco was a general standby, and might be either in Doncaster Works or carrying out conventional duties. Unless the King's Cross A4 had to be replaced on the morning train from Newcastle, engine No 3 would, as soon as the 'Jubilee' had departed, be available for other important duties. It could, for instance, and sometimes did, take forward the Leeds–Glasgow 'Diner' from Newcastle to Edinburgh and also the return working in the evening. I believe that on this turn it would go as far as York with the up train, before returning to Newcastle at the end of the day.

5 Return to Ireland and back to the Great Northern

In the late summer of 1937 our family returned to Ireland and settled in Rostrevor in south County Down, which, since that pleasant Mourne village is only two miles from Warrenpoint, gave ample scope for my early interest in the Great Northern not only to flourish, but to expand.

During my four years in Edinburgh, I had come and gone to Dublin and to Bray but not to any other Irish locality, and hence had had little opportunity to keep up with Irish railway developments between 1933 and 1937. However I did become aware of the new '670' 0-6-2Ts on the South Eastern, of the first two Drumm battery sets, and of the new steel-panelled suburban stock on the GSR. I do not remember seeing my first examples of modern Great Northern coaches until 1937, three months before my permanent return to Ireland, and though I was well aware of the advent of the 'Moguls' and of the North 'Atlantic' coaches on the NCC, it was to be some years before I saw any examples of either. The reason for this latter deprivation (and whatever one may have thought about the North 'Atlantics', it was certainly a deprivation not to have seen the 'Moguls' in their early years) was that when travelling between Edinburgh and Dublin I almost invariably went by 'long sea'.

There were two reasons for this choice of route: first, because I was as interested in ships as I was in railways, and second, because Glasgow–Dublin direct was the cheapest route. The sixteen-day return fare between Dublin and Edinburgh, travelling first class on the ship and third class rail, was 33s (£1.65) – even an impecunious student could afford to purchase a ticket at that price from time to time. The form of these tickets was interesting,

being a series of coupons attached to each other vertically. Thus the Dublin–Edinburgh return had four coupons covering, respectively, the Dublin to Glasgow, Glasgow to Edinburgh, Edinburgh to Glasgow, and Glasgow to Dublin sections of the double journey. If, instead of travelling from Dublin to Glasgow by the direct ship, one went via Belfast, the coupon series was Dublin to Belfast, Belfast to Glasgow, Glasgow to Edinburgh, Edinburgh to Glasgow, Glasgow to Belfast, and Belfast to Dublin. One could travel by either LMS or LNER between Glasgow and Edinburgh, but unless specially asked for, tickets were always issued via LMS. Since all returns between the two Scottish cities were available by either route, one could always travel by LNER for at least one of the intercity journeys and thus have a much greater variety of loco power available than on the ex-Caledonian line.

It is now time to leave our consideration of cross-channel routes, fares and tickets, and renew our acquaintance with the GNR(I). Before doing so, however, we should remember that if rail and sea fares in the 1930s were low, so were railwaymen's wages – a driver of some years standing having a basic weekly wage of around £3.00, whilst on the Great Northern, at any rate, a senior passenger guard's basic figure was a few pence below £3.00.

My detailed knowledge of the Great Northern dates from the summer of 1937, since from that time onwards I made frequent journeys on the Warrenpoint branch and on the main line, activities which only ceased as regards the branch when it closed, and for the main line when I left Ireland in 1989. Soon after World War Two, I came to know the Derry Road almost as well as I knew the back of my own hand, but more of that later. A paradox as regards Great Northern passenger services was that although the company's headquarters were in Dublin, and the main line was 'down' from that city, and 'up' from Belfast, it was the latter city that was the more important from the operating point of view. The only long-distance passenger trains from Dublin were the Belfast expresses, whereas Belfast ran through services to Dublin, Derry and Cavan, as well as having much more in the way of local and outer suburban services. The importance of Belfast for passenger services was reflected in the public timetable sheets displayed at stations. One of these covered the main line, Dublin locals and the 'Irish North'; two others, entitled 'Trains to Belfast' and 'Trains from Belfast', dealt with everything else. (Naturally there was some overlapping.) The Hill of Howth tramway was shown on a small separate sheet.

An almost forgotten aspect of the display of public timetables was that in both Ireland and Britain the various companies had their separate boards (often used for posters as well as time sheets), headed with their names or initials. It was usual for railways to have 'foreign' boards as well as their own at stations, and strict instructions laid down that 'foreign' matter was not to be exhibited on home boards. These boards were usually rectangular, but Great Northern ones were often curved at the top, where they showed the company's title in full except that '(I)' rather than '(Ireland)' was used. As well as boards from the Great Southern and NCC, GNR(I) stations often had LMS and LNER ones. So far as I remember the LMS exhibited posters only, but sometimes on the boards of their East Coast rivals one saw timetables for the Dublin – Isle of Man – Silloth shipping service, and its London and North Eastern connections.

An interesting point in regard to the Great Northern's public timetable booklets, was that the summary tables at the front showed that the main route between Belfast and Enniskillen was via Clones rather than via Omagh, as became the case during and after World War Two. In the 1930s, passengers using either route had to change at one or other of the just-mentioned junctions, though small vans, under customs seal, ran between Belfast and Enniskillen. These vans, and those operating between Dublin and Cavan, gave rise to much shunting activity at Clones. This was because they were conveyed on trains running between Belfast and Cavan and Dundalk and Enniskillen.

As an example of conditions at Clones passenger station in 1938, it might be interesting to look at the period between 17.24 and 17.55 on any weekday. The 15.10 Belfast to Cavan train was due at Clones at 17.24 and was timed to leave at 17.55, whilst in the opposite direction the 16.50 Cavan to Belfast was due in at 17.27 and out at 17.55. Meanwhile, the 16.25 Dundalk to Enniskillen was scheduled for a 17.40 arrival and 17.51 departure, and the 16.47 Enniskillen to Dundalk arrived at 17.30 and left at 17.40. For good measure, the trains from and to Belfast were 'mixed as required' between Cavan and Clones, and in each direction engines were changed at the latter station. To make matters that little bit more difficult, there were only three platforms to accommodate the four trains, one of which had to undergo customs examination. The intense activity generated by the exchange of vans and dealing with the vehicles of the mixed trains, not to mention directing passengers to their correct trains, is not difficult to envisage.

The Warrenpoint Branch

I have implied that my return to Ireland led to a detailed knowledge of the Great Northern main line and of the Warrenpoint branch, so let us take a look at these sections of the railway in 1937–39, starting with the branch. One consequence of my coming to live near Warrenpoint was that I renewed my acquaintance with 4-4-2T No 189, which I had so often seen on the Howth branch in the early 1920s. This engine, and a couple of the newer tank engines of Class T2 (No 189 was a T1) operated virtually all the weekday passenger services on the branch. The general pattern of services was for sets of two bogies to work between Warrenpoint, Newry and Goraghwood, with some trains running to and from Portadown. Connections were made with up and down Belfast trains at Goraghwood, in some cases by through carriages from and to Belfast. In the summer of 1938 there were four of these vehicles each way per day, all but one of which were attached to Dublin expresses between Belfast and 'the Wood'. The exception was the coach which might have been expected to leave Belfast on the 17.40 up Mail. However, as this latter train did not stop at Goraghwood, the through vehicle operated on the 17.45 Belfast–Portadown service. At the latter station it was attached to the branch train which brought it 'all stations' to Warrenpoint. There were five through passenger trains each weekday between Dublin and Belfast but, as mentioned, only four through carriage services between Belfast and Warrenpoint.

The mainline trains which did not convey these coaches were the up and down Mails and the 19.10 up semi-fast. This latter train stopped at Castlebellingham, Dromin, Dunleer, Balbriggan, Skerries and Donabate, as well as the six more usual major stops, and so can scarcely be called an express. Since the up Mail did not call at Goraghwood, passengers from Warrenpoint and Newry by this service to Drogheda and Dublin were brought to Dundalk by GNR(I) bus from Newry (Dublin Bridge), thereby being deprived of the more than spirited running down the south side of the Wellington bank which was usual with the up Mail at that time. On Sundays there was no connection from the Warrenpoint branch into the evening up Dublin train, and one travelled all the way from Newry to Dublin by 'road motor', as the GNR(I) buses were still officially designated.

On the face of it, four through carriages each way per day between Belfast and Warrenpoint, plus connections from and to the branch train when it ran to Portadown, might seem to have been quite a generous provision of facilities for the inhabitants of south Down; however, there were a couple of snags as regards the through carriages. These latter vehicles were brake tri-compos, seating 12 first and 12 second class passengers in compartments, and 38 third class in centre-corridor accommodation. They had no lavatories, and when attached to the mainline trains (at the back on up services and at the front on down ones) the corridor doors were often kept locked, and sometimes indeed the shutters were not removed, thus precluding easy access to the buffet and restaurant cars as well as to other, at times more urgently needed, facilities. It should hardly be necessary to add that, being a railway enthusiast and wise in my generation, I very soon learned to make use of stops at intermediate stations to change vehicles, as and when required, thus circumventing the base plans of shunters and guards to effect my death by starvation or other painful cause.

Although goods traffic on the branch was not as heavy as it had been before the 1933 strike, general merchandise from Belfast and stout from Dublin, together with coal from Newry (and to a certain extent from Warrenpoint), produced some revenue. There was a daily goods each way between Portadown and Newry, and a down mixed and an up goods between Newry and Warrenpoint, together with an evening goods from Newry to Goraghwood, the engine of which returned light to Newry. Special goods trains, mainly carrying coal, operated as required to Markethill over the truncated Goraghwood–Armagh line. Coal trains ex-Newry to other destinations, and cattle trains to that town en route for shipment to Holyhead via Greenore, were examples of other 'as required' services.

An interesting thrice-weekly goods service left Goraghwood at 09.35 for Bessbrook, with a return working at 10.00. This involved Newry, in that the locomotive came up from Newry as pilot on the 09.15 Newry–Portadown passenger train and returned light to the shed from Goraghwood at 10.20.

Another infrequent but regular goods working was the pig train from Banbridge to Newry on Wednesdays, which was scheduled to pass Goraghwood at 14.25 and to arrive at Newry ten minutes later. The train was worked by a Portadown engine and brake van which departed from Newry at 15.00 for their home station. The reason for operating the pig train, which involved running 34½ non-revenue producing miles out of a total of 52, was probably to convey stock from Banbridge pig market to the bacon factory at Newry and also to the Greenore boat.

The just mentioned short workings to and from Bessbrook were in order to avoid having to stop mainline goods trains, and to provide customs facilities at that station. So far as I am aware, the Bessbrook goods traffic comprised only beer from MacArdles brewery at Dundalk, and returned empty casks. MacArdles rented the goods store at Bessbrook, from where they distributed their products to the Newry area. The distance from Dundalk to Newry by road is 12 miles. To convey a cask of beer from the brewery to Newry by rail entailed the following: first an approximately one mile journey from MacArdle's siding near the Dundalk South cabin to the junction goods station, then 17½ miles by mainline goods to Goraghwood, and then two and a half miles back up the bank to Bessbrook, about 21 rail miles in all, involving the use of three different locomotives and their crews. Finally, of course, the beer had to be carried (in 1937–39 by horse and cart) two miles down the road to Newry. I never thought to ask anyone in the Traffic or Accountant's departments of the railway company what was

the net profit on the conveyance of a hogshead of ale from MacArdle's Brewery to Bessbrook. The answer could well have been interesting.

Newry shed, which adjoined Edward Street station, always had several small 0-6-0s – QGs, PGs and ALs – for working not only the regular and special goods trains but also the two ballast trains which were stabled at Goraghwood, where the quarry which supplied ballast for the entire GNR(I) system was situated. Another occasional duty of the 0-6-0s was hauling a stock special on the Greenore line, if the quota of cattle wagons on the tail of the Monday, Wednesday and Saturday mixed train was too great for the GNR(I) 2-4-2Ts and the DNGR 0-6-0STs to cope with, and the regular goods was also fully loaded.

A railbus normally worked all the Greenore–Newry weekday passenger services, except for the mixed trains on the days the Holyhead steamer operated. Another railbus regularly seen in the Newry area was the one which reopened the Banbridge–Scarva branch after the 1933 strike. The bus made a few trips each day between Scarva and Goraghwood, where a light turntable was installed between the branch and the main line on the Newry side of the cabin. By 1937, a railcar (usually 'A') had taken over this service and the turntable was no longer needed, though it remained in place for many years and was in regular use for a short time about 1945–46, as will be recounted later.

Most locomotives seen on the Warrenpoint branch on weekdays were from Newry shed. On summer Sundays, however, matters were very different, with Belfast engines working through trains to Warrenpoint, and machines from Portadown bringing in trains from there and also from Monaghan. Almost any class of loco, other than a 'Compound' or a shunting tank, was liable to turn up at Warrenpoint on a Sunday, though if it was an S class 4-4-0 it had to have a short wheelbase tender, in order to be easily accommodated on the Warrenpoint

Class QL 4-4-0 No 128 of the GNR(I) at Navan on the Drogheda–Oldcastle branch in 1953, the last year of the independent existence of the Great Northern. The QLs were very much the cinderella locomotives of the GNR(I) after about 1921. They were the largest passenger engines permitted to work on the Oldcastle branch.

A Donaldson, courtesy JD Fitzgerald

turntable. This matter of the turntable produced an interesting loco working if an excursion from Dublin was made up to more than seven bogies, which was the limit for a QL 4-4-0 between Dundalk and Goraghwood. In such a case, the S or V ('Compound') engine would come off at Goraghwood and run to Portadown for turning. The train would be worked in both directions on the branch by a loco from Newry shed.

Perhaps the most interesting of all the summer Sunday operations was that of the regular Belfast–Greenore train which stopped only at Lisburn, Lurgan and Portadown between Belfast and Newry, and was timed at normal express speeds over the main line. In company with the up Mail, and certain Sunday Belfast–Dublin expresses which in winter stopped at Bessbrook, it was one of the very few trains scheduled to run through Goraghwood. The Banbridge pig train was also

a member of this exclusive company. The most usual sort of engine for the Belfast–Greenore train would be a PP 4-4-0, and between first arrival at, and final departure from, Greenore the loco and coaches would make an additional Greenore–Newry return trip.

The reason for all these Sunday workings was that in the 1930s (and for many years afterwards) pubs in Northern Ireland were not open (at least officially) on Sundays. However, Ulster thirsts could be slaked on Sundays at Omeath and Carlingford in the Irish Free State, each of which oases was served by the Greenore trains, although Omeath received most of its traffic via Warrenpoint and the ferry boats.

The establishment of the border caused a lot of headaches for the GNR(I), but at least the Sunday trains to Warrenpoint and Greenore (not to mention Bundoran) provided some compensatory revenue.

Let us now take a look at the main line, on which the passenger services can be divided into seven groups. There were, first, the through Dublin–Belfast expresses, five each way on weekdays and three on Sundays; next, the Howth branch trains; and third, the locals between Dublin, Malahide, Drogheda and Dundalk; the fourth group comprised the locals between Belfast and Lisburn; the fifth was made up of stopping trains from Belfast to Banbridge and Newcastle, Antrim and Portadown; whilst the sixth covered through workings to the Cavan and Derry lines from Belfast; and last of all were the Portadown–Newry–Warrenpoint workings which have already been referred to.

Dublin–Belfast Expresses

The through services between Dublin and Belfast were worked by five sets of carriages and normally required five engines in steam each weekday. Three of the carriage sets and three of the locos were based in Dublin, the remainder in Belfast. Engine crews were usually changed at Dundalk, men from Amiens Street, Dundalk and Adelaide sheds sharing the workings. Guards generally worked through from terminus to terminus. South of Dundalk the enginemen's rosters included some duties on the Dublin–Dundalk locals. In 1938 both S and V 4-4-0s were used on the expresses; the first rebuilt Ss came out in that year – Nos 173, 192, and 172 and in that order, with Nos 173 and 192 allocated to Amiens Street shed. In the summer of that year No 173 was the regular engine for the down and up Mails, No 192 was on the 12.00 down and 19.10 up, whilst the 09.00 down and 14.45 up were 'Compound' workings. When No 191 appeared in 1939, she went on the Mails and No 173 took over the 09.00 and 14.45. However, even with the three renewed engines

In 1963, five years after the break-up of the remains of the Great Northern, that company's practice of changing the engines of Belfast–Derry trains at Portadown could still be seen in operation on busy days in summer, when extras to the regular diesel-powered services were run. Here we have Ulster Transport Authority No 58 (formerly GNR(I) No 208 Lagan*) making off to Portadown shed after bringing the 17.00 Belfast–Derry train to Portadown. To the right stands ex-GNR(I) S class No 170* Errigal, *minus name plates, about to take the train on over the switchback road to Derry.* JD Fitzgerald

The sequel to the scene in the last illustration; No 170 ready to depart for Derry. On this occasion the author was on the footplate. JD Fitzgerald

The author turns his back on Portadown as No 170 sets off for Derry on 13 July 1963. I hasten to assure older readers, who may remember the unflattering allusions to Portadown expressed in graffiti* in the toilet compartments of GNR(I) coaches in bygone days, that no political, religious, or any other inference should be drawn from my position. JD Fitzgerald

(* "Do not use the lavatory while the train is standing at a station. – *except at Portadown*")

in regular operation, a 'Compound' was normally shedded at Amiens Street. I can remember, for instance, a 'Compound' working the down Sunday 10.30 at least once during December 1938.

Adelaide engines were responsible for the 08.15 and 10.30 up and the 15.15 and 18.40 down trains. Until the autumn of 1938 these were normally 'Compound' turns, but during the 1938–39 winter, and as more rebuilt locos became available, an 'S' often appeared on the 10.30 and the return working at 15.15. Once, in July 1938, I saw No 172 at Portadown on the 10.30 – the load ex-Belfast was heavy, with nine for Dublin, two for Derry (off at Portadown) and one for Warrenpoint (off at Goraghwood). The train engine had a Q 4-4-0 as pilot at least as far as Portadown, though how far beyond Portadown this latter loco went I do not know. Even in winter the renewed S and S2 engines were not so often used on the 08.15 and 18.40 trains; the former regularly loaded to 11 or 12 bogies between Belfast and Portadown and the latter to eight (plus a loaded 20-ton P van) between Drogheda and Dundalk. On some summer evenings this train would comprise ten bogies ex Dublin, with the P van still being added at Drogheda.

Although the down train was not usually unduly heavy, it had cross-channel boat and mail connections at either end of its journey, and the extra engine power on the Wellington and Kellystown banks was helpful in maintaining the tight schedules involved.

The commonest basic make-up of a Dublin–Belfast set was six bogies marshalled as follows from north to south: brake third, two thirds, restaurant or buffet car, first/second compo, brake second. There were, however, minor modifications to this pattern in some of the sets. The 06.40 down and 17.40 up (the Mail set) had a brake first/third instead of a brake third at the north end. This coach worked between Dun Laoghaire Pier and Belfast, connecting with the Holyhead steamer service. Additionally, a bogie van, for cross-channel mails and customs sealed luggage between Britain and Northern Ireland, ran between the Pier and Belfast. This van was marshalled in front of the through first/third, ie immediately behind the engine, in the down direction. There was no brake third on the 08.15 up and 18.40 down, its place being taken by a bogie van which worked from Dun Laoghaire Pier with cross-channel mails from the daylight steamer from Holyhead. Although this van came up from Belfast on the 08.15 each day, the morning steamer from Dun Laoghaire left too early to permit of a through day Mail service from Belfast to London. Very often this 08.15/18.40 set had three full thirds, though on midweek winter days there might be only two. The two carriage sets which worked the 09.00 down/14.45 up and the 10.30 up/15.15 down were more often than not composed of the basic six-bogie formation. The fifth set, used on the 12.00 down and 19.10 up, was the 'odd man out'. During 1937–39 its make-up was, from north to south, brake first, restaurant car, second/third compo, third, brake third.

Each of the five sets conveyed through carriages to and from places off the main line. The 09.00, 15.15 and 18.40 down and the 08.15, 14.45 and 17.40 up had through carriages between Dublin and Enniskillen (off and on at Dundalk). In summer, the first two of these down, and the last two up, operated to and from Bundoran. All down trains except the Mail, together with the 08.15, 10.30 and 14.45 up, had Belfast–Warrenpoint coaches, whilst the 15.15 down and 14.45 up were the trains to which the Dublin–Derry through brake tricompos were attached. The attachment of a Warrenpoint through coach to the 17.45 ex-Belfast, rather than to the 17.40 Dublin train, has already been explained.

Completing the list of through carriages conveyed by mainline expresses were the four bogies (plus a small van for Enniskillen) for Cavan, on the back of the 08.15 and 19.10 up trains between Belfast and Portadown and the two Belfast–Derry bogies on the 10.30 up, also as far as Portadown. Whilst the 08.15 up express regularly loaded to 11 or 12 bogies and a van ex-Belfast, a comparable load was also taken out of Great Victoria Street on certain days during the summer by the 10.30. The 12 vehicles would comprise the normal six-bogie set, plus an extra third for Dublin, together with a restaurant car and a tabled third for specially booked tourist parties for the same destination. Behind these nine vehicles would be the regular brake tri-compo for Warrenpoint and two bogies for Derry.

The first examples of 'modern' GNR(I) passenger stock (flush sided, steel panelled and with wide windows) appeared in 1935, and by 1938 there was a number of these vehicles available for the mainline expresses. In the four larger sets all the thirds, together with the first/second compos, were generally of the new type, whilst on the remaining set (12.00 ex-Dublin and 19.10 ex-Belfast) the full third was also a modern coach. The pioneer brake third of the new series came from the works towards the end of 1937, but after operating for a while in the 10.30/15.15 set it was transferred to work between Belfast and Cavan. With its six 'compartments' (centre-corridor sections) it did not have sufficient van accommodation for the mainline workings. The first of what were to be three modern brake tri-compos (No 47) also dated from 1937, and from its introduction it worked regularly between Dublin and Derry. However, it was 1942, so far as I can remember, before all three of these new brake tri-compos were in operation.

Despite their contemporary external appearance, the new mainline thirds were the direct descendants of the older wooden-bodied centre-corridor stock which I described when detailing my first Derry line journey, for they perpetuated two of the less attractive features of those somewhat less than ideal vehicles. First, though seating 70 passengers, they had only one toilet per coach, and second, they retained the four doors per side of the earlier design, thus providing a wide window for only every second section of seats.

However, the two regular thirds in the Mail set, Nos 66 and 67, were of the side-corridor type, with eight compartments and one toilet per coach. These latter vehicles had particularly comfortable seats, but were short on leg room.

The new first/second compos were thoroughly up to date vehicles, side-corridor with four first and three second class compartments, which, with three-a-side seating in the firsts and four in the seconds, provided a total of 48 seats. There were lavatory compartments at each end. Mathematically minded readers should not find it difficult to calculate by exactly what percentage the ratio of toilet facilities to seats in 'superior class' accommodation exceeded the figure for the third class. All compartments in these compos, seconds as well as firsts, had warm-air heating. Vehicles built from 1940 onwards, however, had conventional steam heating.

Another later regression in standards (due, like the changed heating methods, to the wartime shortage of materials) was the substitution of wood fibre panelling for the steel panelling of the original 'modern' coaches. One did not give it much thought at the time, but I have often wondered since what would have been the extent of the damage, and the number of casualties, had one or more of these later vehicles been involved in a serious accident.

Finally, as regards the new coaches, a prominent feature was the large headboards with black relief block letters reading 'Dublin–Belfast' and vice versa (later also 'Belfast–Derry'), which were mounted on the sides of the roofs. Similar boards, but with red lettering and the words 'Restaurant Car' or

'Buffet Car', were carried on the catering vehicles, and in this case on old as well as new stock. I have a stray recollection regarding destination boards. When the pioneer 'new' brake third was transferred from the main line to the Belfast–Cavan service the word 'Dublin' on the roof boards was obscured, but not 'Belfast', which latter word, with all the emphasis of its large letters, remained in place. This must have been rather confusing to non-railway-minded travellers when the vehicle was on its way to Cavan. In later years this coach, and others of the same design, had one section of seats converted to van accommodation, making them suitable for mainline service.

All other stock, except for some catering vehicles used in the mainline sets, was of the standard pre-1935 wooden type. The only feature calling for attention was that the four- and five-compartment brake seconds were downgraded firsts, dating from the 1920s.

Finally, as regards the mainline sets, a few words about the catering vehicles. There were five cars in regular use, and except for the introduction of No 88 dining car in 1938, and two changes in the rostering of cars as the result of this, all cars ran in the same sets from 1937 to 1940. In the former year the two newest vehicles were buffet cars Nos 266 and 267, built in 1936, and which ran in the 09.00/14.45 and 10.30/15.15 trains. These cars each had accommodation for 40 passengers, seated at tables for four on tubular metal-framed chairs. Towards one end of each car was a bar, and beyond it a small kitchen in which simple cooking by compressed gas could be undertaken. The gas used was ordinary town gas, supplied under considerable pressure (in cylinders) by Belfast Corporation Gasworks. Its use was extended to other Great Northern catering stock, but was discontinued in favour of 'bottle gas' from commercial sources after a serious explosion in a tea car at Cavan. Each buffet car had a door on either side at the end remote from the kitchen, but

there was no partition between the seating accommodation and the entrance space. The cars were fitted with Clayton hot-air heaters.

Despite their rather cramped seating accommodation, Nos 266 and 267 became very popular. Almost any change from the former tea tray service to passengers in their seats would have been an improvement, but with the introduction of the new buffet cars the Great Northern had, in one move, progressed from barely basic to thoroughly up to date catering facilities for all types of service, other than heavy main meals.

Until the introduction of No 88 (happily still extant under the ownership of the Railway Preservation Society of Ireland, though internally much changed from her original form), by far the most attractive car in use on the main line was restaurant car No 401, which ran in the Mail set. This vehicle was built at Dundalk in 1916, as one of a pair of conventional wooden-panelled diners, to the standard elliptical-roofed profile and overall dimensions of 58'0" x 9'6". Accommodation was provided for 15 first class passengers in the centre of the car and 19 second class at one end. Seating in each class was provided by substantial wooden chairs, well upholstered and with the company's initials carved at the top of the seat backs. For the first time on the Great Northern, end kitchens were provided.

No 401 was in the train which was derailed at Dromiskin during the strike early in 1933, and the car was severely damaged, necessitating extensive rebuilding. The vehicle was taken in hand by the works immediately, and reappeared later in the same year considerably changed in both external appearance and internal layout. The first and second accommodation was interchanged, first now being at one end and second in the centre, though there was no alteration in the number of seats provided in each class. The wooden chairs were also retained. The walls of the first class saloon were covered with 'rexine', a synthetic leather-like material much in vogue at the time, and the tables were given individual lights and silver-plated (possibly electro-plated) flower vases. The second (formerly first) class saloon was less altered and retained its polished woodwork. Clayton heaters were provided for each saloon.

Despite these internal changes, the most striking alterations in the post-strike No 401 concerned the windows. Wooden panels between the main wide windows were removed and replaced by oval windows, which produced a feeling of airiness and spaciousness and gave the car a character markedly different from that of any other GNR(I) catering vehicle.

The sister car, No 402, was never altered. For some years, up to the summer of 1938, it ran in the 08.15 up and 18.40 down trains, but as soon as No 88 came into service No 402 was transferred to the 12.00 ex-Dublin/19.10 ex-Belfast train. This latter working had hitherto operated with car No 144, a centre-kitchen vehicle which had been built as an inspection car in 1916 and was subsequently twice altered, first, in 1927, to an all-third centre-kitchen diner, and again, in 1934, to first and second. In this final form, the car catered for 11 first and 22 second class diners in separate saloons on either side of the kitchen. No 144 was unique among Great Northern centre-kitchen restaurant cars, in having a high elliptical, rather than a clerestory, roof.

The new diner, No 88, was thoroughly up to date in most of its internal arrangements, including an end kitchen, but it reverted to fixed seats rather than the free-standing chairs of all other purpose-built restaurant and buffet cars from 1916 onwards. However, with two plus one seating in each class, and a total of 18 seconds and 12 firsts (the latter at one end of the car), No 88 provided ample room for its patrons, appreciably more than was available in the 40-seater buffet cars of two years earlier. But maybe the three- and four-course

breakfasts and five-course dinners served in No 88 called for wider seats and more leg room than did the fries and other less substantial snacks on offer in the buffet cars.

There were three other dining cars on the Great Northern in late pre-war days, one of which from time to time would appear as a relief on the mainline services, and in summer as one of the two special tourist vehicles on the 10.30 up and 18.40 down trains. These cars were Nos 409, 427 and 457, which dated from 1895, 1900 and 1905 respectively. They were all built to the standard clerestory-roofed centre-kitchen pattern of their day. Since by the later 1930s they were not in regular mainline service they need not further concern us here.

Two almost forgotten types of catering vehicle, which from time to time appeared on the main line during the late 1930s and very early 1940s, were the small buffet cars and the 'beer wagons'. The former were adaptations of standard third class wooden coaches, from which seats were removed at one end to form small saloons seating 12 people on chairs, plus very basic cooking facilities. These cars were Nos 238 and 239, centre-corridor Class K12, and No 295, side-corridor Class K14. On the main line one of these was regularly included in the summer Saturdays-only 09.20 relief to the 09.00 down, which conveyed through coaches from Dublin to Bangor, Newcastle and Portrush. On Mondays to Fridays the Portrush coach was attached to the regular 09.00 train and was slipped at Lisburn, but the Saturday relief train stopped at the latter station, where not only the through Portrush vehicle(s) but also the buffet car were detached. The car went as far as Antrim, whence it returned on the balancing up service to Dublin. Apart from a wartime exception, to be referred to later, this must have been the only regularly scheduled working of a catering vehicle over the Antrim branch.

Mention of the Dublin–Newcastle through coach on the Saturday 09.20 down relief train reminds me that although this latter was never a particularly heavy train a pilot loco was provided from Dundalk to Goraghwood, not specifically as an assisting engine but in order to take forward the Newcastle coach from Goraghwood. On the return journey this engine piloted a Newcastle–Belfast train (to which the Dublin coach was attached) as far as Banbridge, and then took the single coach through non-stop to Dundalk where it was attached to the 14.45 ex-Belfast, which latter train on Saturdays ran non-stop to Dundalk.

To get back to mainline catering vehicles – a small buffet car was used as required to relieve Nos 266 and 267 in the 09.00/14.45 and 10.30/15.15 trains. Mention of the classification of the small cars, K12 and K14, also reminds me that whereas, in the annual returns and statements of accounts of the Great Northern, which had to be made in the forms prescribed by law, 'restaurant cars' were enumerated under that heading, all buffet vehicles, including the new Nos 266 and 267, were shown under the classification 'Carriages of uniform class – third class.'

All dining cars (classification letter B) had first and second class accommodation only. Third class passengers were graciously permitted to partake of both solid and liquid refreshment in the second class saloons – after all, their money was as good as anyone else's, but it was laid down in the appendices to the working timetables that these 'inferior types' had to be sent back to their humble seats as soon as they had finished their meals. In my experience, however, the staffs were not too rigorous in applying this regulation. Many are the Great Northern miles I have travelled on a third class ticket in the superior accommodation of a second class dining saloon, with just a cup of tea or coffee as my excuse for desecrating the second class precincts with my third class presence. For instance, if I joined the 08.15 ex-Belfast at Goraghwood and it was not possible to find a

corner seat at one of the restricted number of wide windows in a K15, I made for the restaurant car immediately on leaving Dundalk, found myself a window corner, and with a judiciously spaced intake of coffee as an excuse, could usually manage to remain there until the staff started clearing up somewhere about Donabate.

I referred earlier to the 'beer wagons'. These were old six-wheeled vans fitted with bars and shelves on which to rest glasses, for use in excursion trains. They did not survive long into the 1940s, as shortage of supplies led to the serving of alcoholic drinks being limited to those passengers who also purchased meals, but while they lasted they attracted some custom. The design (if it can be so called) of these conversions was based closely on that of similar adaptations of old vans on the GSR. Indeed, the Chief Draughtsman at Dundalk told me that when consideration was being given to introducing 'beer wagons', he one day boarded a through cross-border excursion from the GSR at Dundalk, quite unofficially and without any prior notice to the authorities at Inchicore, in order to ascertain what was required and the work involved.

Catering services were an aspect of railway operation that greatly interested me in Great Northern days, but since I have written extensively on both GNR(I) and GSR dining and buffet cars in IRRS Journals, I will not go further into the subject here.

The Howth Branch

Next for consideration is the Howth branch, which, so far as steam trains were concerned, showed no great change from the position in the early 1920s, although there were some rather more modern (though still wooden) coaches in use. Motive power was still provided by the 1–5 series of T2 4-42T engines, plus some of the Tls (Nos 185–189), though, as has been mentioned, No 189 was now at Newry. There was, however, a major

This photograph of GNR(I) articulated railcar C2 at Cavan clearly shows the division of Cavan passenger station between the Great Southern and the Great Northern railways. The station was owned by the 'Southern' but regularly used by the 'Northern' which had no passenger station of its own at Cavan. The railcar is in the Northern bay whilst a GSR goods brake van is in the Southern one. The through road is to the right of the island platform and the cattle dock and siding are on the far right.

EM Patterson, JD Fitzgerald collection

innovation in the form of the triplet railcars. These cars, designated *D, E, F* and *G*, were developed from the earlier *A, B, C1, C2* and *C3*, and particularly from the last two, which cars, with the front ends of their passenger-carrying sections articulated to the power bogies, were designed to operate back to back as a single unit. *C2* and *C3* did indeed commence their working life on the Dublin–Malahide and Dublin–Howth routes, but after a couple of years left the suburban services, never to return. For most of the rest of their lives these two cars worked as separate vehicles in the Dundalk – Clones – Bundoran – Omagh – Portadown area, where for the most part C1 was also to be found.

Although *C2* and *C3* were interesting in themselves, and even more so as marking a stage in the extensive development of railcars

by the Great Northern, they were of only minor importance for the Howth branch. Matters were very different, however, as regards *D, E, F* and *G*. From the introduction of the first two in 1936, until their supercession by the AEC cars in the 1950s, there were always two of the vehicles stationed in Dublin, from where they operated most non-rush-hour Howth trains and also ran to and from Killester, Malahide and Balbriggan. A total of 13 out of 21 Monday to Friday Howth trains were worked by railcars, as were a number of services which terminated variously at one or other of the three just mentioned mainline stations. As soon as *F* and *G* came into use, they replaced *D* and *E* at Dublin. One of the earlier cars then went to Belfast for suburban service, whilst the other, when not relieving at either mainline terminus, carried out various duties, including for a time running between Newry and

Goraghwood. In the winter of 1939–40, this Newry-based car was out of action for a while due to a burst radiator (or possibly cylinder block), incurred when lying outside the shed on a particularly cold night.

Although the four triplet units had a fairly close outward resemblance, there were considerable differences between each pair. Each was double ended, with passenger accommodation at either end of a power unit to which the accommodation sections were articulated. However, this was as far as the mechanical similarity went. *D* and *E* had a six-coupled centre section, to which power was supplied by a single 153 hp Gardner engine. (At the time the GNR(I) built its own buses and used Gardner engines exclusively.) The centre power section not only housed the engine, but also provided guard's accommodation. *F* and *G* were more powerful – 204 hp – and had four-wheeled engine sections with individual drive to each axle. Their guards no longer had to travel beside the engine rooms, but had a separate compartment at the inner end of one of the passenger saloons. *D* and *E* had seats for 159, while *F* and *G* had seating for 164 passengers. In each of the four units one saloon was entirely third class, with three plus two fixed bus-type seats on either side of a central corridor. The other saloon, for most of its length, was designated second class. It had the same seating arrangements as the third, and I could never discern any difference between the two classes other than that the 'second' seats were upholstered in blue material and the thirds in brown.

Towards the inner end of the mainly second class saloon was a single first class compartment, with its own side doors and two plus two seating. Whether any passengers, other than senior officers of the Great Northern, some of whom lived between Clontarf and Howth and on the Hill, ever used these first class compartments, I do not know.

Finally, there was a short third class section between the 'first' compartment and the extreme inner end of this saloon.

These four diesel units were appreciably lower in height than the standard passenger stock, though of much the same width, and were of lightweight construction, approximating to contemporary bus standards. Like all other railcars of the company, they were painted in the blue and cream of the road passenger fleet. The ends of the cars were rounded, with three windows, behind the centre one of which was a narrow driver's compartment. As well as the separate doors for the first class compartment, each saloon had two doors per side, making a total of 12 for each articulated unit.

Mainline Locals

So much for the Howth branch. Local services on the main line from Dublin comprised the railcar workings already mentioned and also steam trains, most of which operated to and from Drogheda. By the time I returned to Ireland, the steam-worked 'push pulls' to Malahide no longer ran.

The Drogheda trains usually consisted of three or four bogie coaches headed by a 4-4-2T, although a PP 4-4-0 would sometimes appear. I remember seeing one of these small tender engines on the 18.15 ex-Amiens Street, a 'semi fast' rather than a conventional 'local', since it ran non-stop to Rush. It would seem likely that this was a Drogheda engine, one of the small 4-4-0s which that shed was allotted, primarily for working the Oldcastle branch passenger trains.

What might be described as long-distance locals ran between Dublin and Dundalk, stopping at all stations from Malahide or Portmarnock onwards, with corresponding up workings. These trains, which were commonly hauled by QL 4-4-0s in the charge of 'top link' Dublin and Dundalk enginemen, were smartly timed. For example, the 07.55 down was

GNR(I) 4-4-0 No 12 of Class PP approaching Kells. Locomotives of this type, based at Drogheda for the Oldcastle branch passenger trains, occasionally appeared on suburban workings between Drogheda and Dublin. Once, in the 1950s, the author saw the 09.00 Dublin–Belfast express running through Derriaghy in the Belfast suburbs headed by two PPs. Presumably the Class V or VS loco rostered for the train had failed somewhere along the line, possibly south of Drogheda, or perhaps between Dundalk and Goraghwood.

JD Fitzgerald collection

allowed 14 minutes start to stop from Drogheda to Dunleer, including the slow start from Drogheda and the climb up Kellystown bank. The four miles from Dromin Junction to Castlebellingham were allowed six minutes. As well as passengers and parcels for the various mainline stations which they served, the Dundalk locals also conveyed through four- and six-wheeled vans for the 'Irish North' and the Cavan and Bundoran lines.

At the northern end of the main line, the Belfast–Lisburn locals had a higher proportion of steam trains than was the case in the Dublin area, and some of these still operated as 'push pulls'. As with Dublin locals, most of the steam motive power was provided by 4-4-2T locos. During the summer of 1938, however, one of the first pair of articulated railcars (whether it was *D* or *E*, I do not now remember) worked ten round trips between Belfast and Lisburn and one Belfast–Banbridge return each day, Monday to Friday.

On Saturdays some of these workings were scheduled for steam operation, so that the railcar could be used for afternoon excursions to Warrenpoint. I once saw a 'triplet' arriving in Warrenpoint on such a working with every seat occupied, including some chairs which had been placed in the wide circulating spaces around the driver's compartments at the outer ends of the saloons. Although I have forgotten the exact wording of the complete announcement, I well remember that these excursions were advertised as being 'by de luxe observation railcar' or some such high-sounding phrase. How accurate this description was felt to be by the passengers sitting for well over an hour on hard upright chairs, as the car jogged along at its maximum 45 mph to the accompanying ring of its coupling rods, is anybody's guess. But then at a fare of around 2s (10p) return, the excursionists had little cause to complain. I never travelled on one of these cheap railcar trips to Warrenpoint, but in the autumn of 1938, when working in Dublin, I once made use of a conventional steam-hauled Sunday excursion to the south Down seaside resort. However, the fare this time was half a crown (12½p).

Many of the stopping trains between Belfast and Banbridge, Portadown and Antrim served all or some of the stations between Belfast and Lisburn, making an end to end journey a long-drawn-out affair. However, in the case of trains making only a few intermediate stops – for example, just Lisburn and Lurgan between Belfast and Portadown – express timings applied. The best of these trains was the 17.45 from Belfast which conveyed through coaches for Warrenpoint and sometimes for Omagh, and was usually made up to a total of four bogies. The most common locomotive type which I saw used was a PP 4-4-0. Working times were 11 minutes for Belfast–Lisburn, 15 minutes for Lisburn–Lurgan, and eight minutes for Lurgan–Portadown. The 15 minutes start to stop for the 12½ miles from Lisburn to Lurgan, which included the climb up to Milepost 96 at the top of the Moira bank, was excellent work and was equalled by only one other regular train, the 19.10 Belfast–Dublin. The engine working this latter service, however, put up the better performance of the two, in that whereas the PP on the 17.45 had only four bogies behind its tender, the S or S2 at the head of the 19.10 would have not only the five vehicles of the mainline set but additionally four bogies and small van (all off at Portadown) for the Cavan line, making its load more than twice as heavy as that of the PP.

Banbridge and Antrim

Engines of Banbridge line trains, some of which ran to and from Newcastle, comprised a mixture of small 4-4-0s, SGs, SG2s and small 0-6-0s. The UG 0-6-0s, which were common on the branch in later years, did not appear until 1937, and I do not remember seeing any of them on the Banbridge line in pre-war days. For the record, the first of these handy little mixed traffic machines which I saw in service was heading the 16.25 Dundalk–Enniskillen, just before Christmas 1937. This loco was one of the first entirely new engines on the GNR(I) since the advent of the last batch of 4-4-2Ts and the 'Compounds'. The UGs, with their side window cabs and high sided tenders, on which appeared the initials GN in large capitals with the company's coat of arms in between (as was the case with the repainted 'Compounds' and the rebuilt Ss and S2s), certainly introduced a new look for Northern 0-6-0s, despite their all-over black paint.

As was often the case on Irish branch lines, the first morning passenger trains from both Newcastle and Antrim were worked by the engines which had brought in the nightly goods. Passenger services on the Antrim branch were sparse, with only four daily services to and from Antrim, an extra as far as Crumlin on Tuesdays, and two additional services to Aldergrove on Saturday evenings, one of which was propelled from Crumlin to Aldergrove. In contrast to the trains to and from Newcastle, for which small engines, either passenger or goods, had to be used owing to weight restrictions south of Banbridge, Antrim trains could be and were powered by larger machines, notably 4-4-2Ts and SG and SG2 0-6-0s.

Two further points regarding the Antrim branch service provide an interesting insight into the traffic conditions of more than half a century ago. The first point concerns the daily up and down goods trains which, as well as conveying whatever traffic was offered to

Antrim itself and through wagons to and from the NCC line (Guinness's products for Ballymena and Coleraine, for example), were booked to call at Ballinderry, Glenavy, Crumlin and Aldergrove in the down direction and at the first three of these stations on the return journey. I suspect, though I cannot be sure since I never saw a 1937–39 Antrim goods (ex-Grosvenor Street yard 04.15 and ex-Antrim at 19.40), that coal to, and linen products from, Crumlin were still providing some traffic.

The second point to note is that the 11.45 passenger Lisburn to Antrim on summer Saturdays was shown in the working timetable as 'Express Passenger'. This train took a connection out of the 11.00 Belfast–Newcastle, and also brought forward the Dublin–Portrush through coach or coaches and the small buffet car for Antrim off the 09.20 down relief express. What this amounted to was that all stops between Lisburn and Antrim, except Ballinderry and Crumlin, were omitted. Since no extra service was provided for the bypassed stations, it is obvious that these can have produced very little traffic. However, since the timetable for the summer of 1938 stated that the Antrim 'Exp Psr' would stop at any of these latter stations to pick up or to set down from stations 'Portadown and beyond', there can scarcely have been much express running.

I only once travelled over the Antrim branch in the 1930s, by the 17.40 ex-Antrim all stations to Belfast (except Millar's Bridge). The latter station consisted of a wheelless covered wagon by the lineside to provide accommodation for the halt keeper, even if not the occasional passenger who may have entrained at this County Antrim metropolis.

The train in which I travelled was composed of three bogie vehicles, including one of the notorious 100-seater thirds. Motive power, as I expected, was a 4-4-2T. My main memory of this journey has nothing to do with the GNR(I), or even the NCC, by which I had journeyed to Antrim from Belfast earlier in the

afternoon. (Return tickets were available by either route, as was the case between Belfast and Cookstown, and Belfast and Derry.) The only other passenger in my compartment was a talkative elderly man who, on learning that I was from Dublin, vouchsafed the statement that Dublin was like Liverpool. I have never been sure whether I was meant to regard this as a compliment or an insult to my native city.

A feature of the Antrim branch passenger traffic, such as it was, was that it was centred on Lisburn rather than Belfast. From Antrim to the latter city was several miles shorter by NCC, and in addition the NCC provided some non-stop services. The distances by road from Crumlin, Aldergrove and Glenavy to Belfast were also considerably shorter than by GNR(I) rail.

Most of the local services between Belfast and Portadown were operated by locomotives from Portadown shed, tank engines again being prominent. The rolling stock, as was the case with other local services, was a very mixed bag, ranging from 100-seat thirds and eight-compartment (later eight and a half-compartment) clerestory-roofed bogie coaches to the relatively modern non-corridor first/second compos, with high elliptical roofs and the tri-compo and brake second varieties of these. These latter vehicles, among the last conventional wooden-panelled coaches to be built at Dundalk, were good looking and comfortable, and were the last to be built for specifically suburban services.

Other types of vehicle to be seen in Belfast–Portadown locals were the ex-rail motor coaches and trailers. These had high arc roofs and were rather longer that the standard Great Northern measurement of 58'0" over headstocks. So far as I remember, their length was 62'0". These were the carriages which, on the Howth branch in the early 1920s, I and my friends referred to as 'observation cars'. The 'observation cars' were more attractive to look at than to ride in. Although they had wide

LMS/NCC U2 class 4-4-0 No 71, Glenarm Castle, on an up train at Monkstown in the northern suburbs of Belfast, in the 1930s. The 'Midlandisation' of the NCC, so apparent in its locos in the inter-war years, did not extend to coaches for secondary services. Note the absence of a coupling on the front draw hook, a feature (or non feature) also seen on the 'Moguls'. W Robb

windows as well as high roofs, the seats were not particularly comfortable, leg room in the third class was restricted, and the windows, which extended to cant rail height and could not be opened, made things very stuffy on summer days. At such times, even a 100-seater dating from the 1890s, with drop lights in the doors, had something to recommend it. One of the ex-rail motors, a brake tri-compo, No 207, was given corridor connections, though no toilet facilities, and occasionally operated in the Belfast–Warrenpoint through carriage service.

Belfast–Derry

The final group of passenger services on the main line to be considered are those between Belfast and Derry and Belfast and Cavan. The Derry trains were interesting in that the long-distance engine workings were often between Portadown and Derry, and vice versa, rather than to and from Belfast. At such

times the trains were powered between Belfast and Portadown by engines which took their turns on the local services. A 4-4-2T heading a Derry train out of Great Victoria Street was by no means an uncommon sight.

Before the NCC opened the Greenisland loop line, the Great Northern had competed with it for Belfast–Derry traffic on fairly even terms. Despite the greater length of the Great Northern route, the tedious reversal procedure at Greenisland added to the overall journey time by the shorter route. However, as soon as the loop line came into operation the GNR(I) was definitely number two for travellers from Belfast to Derry. In the later 1930s this was reflected in the timetable, which provided only four through weekday service trains and no through city to city connection at all on Sundays. It was theoretically possible during the period of operation of the summer timetable to leave Belfast at 09.50 on a Sunday and, by dint of changing at Portadown,

Dungannon (two hours wait) and Omagh (nine hours wait), arrive in Derry at 23.00, but it seems unlikely that even a dedicated railway enthusiast ever essayed that particular journey. Even on weekdays the last through service ex-Belfast left at 16.45, though it was possible to make a later departure by travelling by the 17.45 and changing at Omagh into an immediately connecting train.

As well as the 16.45, the other trains from Belfast through to Derry were the 08.25 (the Mail), the 10.30 and the 13.30. In the reverse direction there were through services from Derry at 07.20, 12.45, 16.10 (Mail) and 19.20. As far as running on the main line was concerned, the 08.25 was allowed only 40 minutes to Portadown, including stops at Lisburn, Moira and Lurgan. This was a respectable performance, considering that on restarting at Moira the engine was immediately faced with the ascent to Milepost 96. The usual load for the Mail leaving Belfast was five bogies, comprising brake third, third, small buffet car (which provided 32 or 40 ordinary seats as well as catering accommodation), first/second compo and bogie van.

The 10.30 ex-Belfast which was attached to the back of the second up morning Dublin express as far as Portadown, to which it was scheduled to run in 30 minutes, had an interesting make-up. The 'train' consisted of a first/second brake compo, No 311 or 312, and a side-corridor tea car adapted from one of the K14 thirds. These latter, the last built of the mainline wooden coaches, were comfortable vehicles with well sprung seats, even though their internal finish was extremely plain. Nos 311 and 312 compos were centre-corridor throughout, with separate first and second class toilet facilities between the two classes of accommodation. There was only one door per side for each class, the sections which did not have doors having wide windows divided by narrow vertical panels. The provision of a tea car in this two-coach formation, which had a

total seating capacity of 92 (12 first, 16 second and 64 third), like the small buffet car on the Antrim branch and the Goraghwood to Bessbrook goods, is another example of how the Great Northern never neglected the opportunity of adding a few more pence to gross receipts. The incentive for providing catering facilities in such a small train was the fact that at Portadown it took a connection out of the 09.00 Dublin–Belfast express.

The 13.25 Belfast–Derry was usually a four-bogie train, comprising two thirds, one of which was a tea car, an old clerestory-roofed first/second and a large van. There might also be one or more small vans on the tail of the train. Finally, the 16.45 from Belfast was a five-piece set, including a small buffet car and a clerestory-roofed first/second.

There is no need to comment further on three of the four Derry line carriage sets, two of which were stabled overnight at each terminus, but two items in connection with the Mails are worth noting. The first point is that these trains conveyed a TPO between Portadown and Derry in each direction. Before the establishment of the border, the TPO operated between Dublin and Derry, when such unlikely places as Malahide and Castlebellingham had had their mails collected and delivered by the apparatus on the side of the vehicle. In its truncated form, the TPO service was continued until World War Two, ensuring that cross-channel mails for Northern Ireland no longer travelled via Holyhead and Dun Laoghaire. However, at the time of which I am writing, mails from Holyhead travelled northwards in the vans at the head of the 06.40 and 18.40 ex-Amiens Street, which have already been referred to. Mails for Derry city and its environs, and Counties Donegal and Tyrone, by the 06.40 were transferred to the TPO at Portadown.

During most of the 1920s, and right up to the outbreak of war, the regular Post Office vehicle was No 790, which had been built about 1921. When the TPO service ceased, No

An unidentified Qs class 4-4-0 (possibly No 136) of the GNR(I) ahead of a black S class 4-4-0 at Great Victoria Street station, Belfast. Despite appearances, the Q may not be about to pilot the S out of Platform 2. The white square over the left-hand buffer shows that the Q was at the back of a two-loco consist which had just come down from Adelaide shed. The Q may be about to be hooked off before going to another platform to head a different train.

JD Fitzgerald collection

790 retired to Dundalk where, after spending many years on the siding beside the former railmotor shop, it was eventually scrapped without ever being used again.

During the operation of the summer timetable the up Derry Mail was an impressive sight by Great Northern standards, as the six or seven bogies would be increased to seven or eight at Omagh by the addition of a through brake tri-compo from Bundoran to Belfast. The tight timings, heavy gradients and numerous restricted curves from which rapid acceleration was called for, meant that an unassisted Qs class 4-4-0 would have been hard pressed to keep to schedule with seven bogies, let along eight. Hence the up Mail was double headed from Omagh to Portadown. Although in the 1930s the train engine was in my experience always a Q, the pilot could be a P or PP or even a second Q.

I have retained many mental pictures of Great Northern activities of 50 and 60 years ago. One of the most vivid is of the Derry Mail, headed by two Q class 4-4-0s, rounding the sharp curve opposite Portadown shed, just before the triple junction of the Dublin, Cavan and Derry lines. With their high-pitched boilers, neat outline and modern tenders (for the most part annexed from SG3 0-6-0s), the rebuilt Qs were among the most impressive Irish engines of their type and size, whilst their performance more than lived up to the promise of their appearance. Vying with the Q class for good looks among four-coupled passenger engines were, in my opinion, the rebuilt GSWR and GSR 321s. At the other extreme were the ex-MGWR locos which had been given extended smokeboxes when superheated.

My second point as regards the Derry Mail is that it was booked to leave Belfast at a time that gave a considerable margin between the arrival of the down Mail ex-Dublin at Portadown and the Derry train's own arrival at the latter station. The wait of approximately 35 minutes at Portadown station for passengers from Dublin to Derry or County Donegal (as compared to virtually no waiting for passengers by the 09.00, and only about five minutes for those who travelled from Éire by the 12.00 ex-Dublin) was in order to allow for possible delay in the arrival of the Mail steamer at Dun Laoghaire, such an event resulting in the late arrival of the mainline Mail at Portadown. Not that delays by the Mail steamer were lightly incurred, as a stringent penalty clause was part of the contract between the postal authorities and the LMS, which ran the vessels.

However, delays to the steamers could occur, and since the 06.40 from Dublin, due into Belfast at 09.10, carried an appreciable commuter traffic from Portadown and Lurgan, provision was made in the working timetable for a special passenger train to run from Portadown in the path of the Mail, if this latter train was operating more than ten minutes late. Should this occur, there were three provisional paths available for the Mail from Portadown forward. One of these paths, omitting the stop at Lurgan, allowed only 29 minutes start to stop, one minute less than the fastest regular Portadown–Belfast timing of 1937–39. Another provision to obviate the consequences of any late running of the down mainline Mail was that the connection into it from Newry and Warrenpoint was made at Portadown, and not at Goraghwood.

Belfast–Cavan

The last aspect of regular mainline passenger traffic to be considered here is the Belfast–Clones–Cavan service where, as was the case with the 10.30 to Derry, some up Dublin expresses were used to convey coaches from Belfast as far as Portadown. The trains concerned were the 08.15 and the 19.10 ex-Great Victoria Street.

As regards the engine rosters for Belfast–Cavan workings, whilst not all engines worked through between the termini there was at least one Belfast–Clones return working by an Adelaide engine. The locomotive on the 15.10 from Belfast ran to Clones, where it made a quick turn round, leaving again for Belfast at the head of the 17.55 train (16.50 from Cavan). Since the 15.10, as has been mentioned earlier, did not arrive in Clones until 17.24, it was only the close proximity of Clones shed and turntable to the passenger station that enabled the quick turn around to be made. I believe that this particular engine working was not invariable, and that sometimes the engine would be booked to work right through to Cavan, returning with the early morning train to Belfast. However, since my first journey between Portadown and Clones did not take place until 1946, I cannot be positive about the loco workings of the 1930s.

What I do remember about engines on Cavan trains is their variety. For example, on two occasions on which I travelled between Portadown and Belfast on the 16.50 ex-Cavan (I had started my journey on the 18.20 Warrenpoint–Portadown train) we had, first in the autumn of 1937, unrebuilt S class 4-4-0 No 170, my old acquaintance from the Howth branch, and second, in the spring of 1938, UG 0-6-0 No 82. This latter occasion provided me with my first experience of travelling behind one of these new light mixed traffic locomotives. The normal year-round passenger service between Belfast and Cavan was four through trains ex-Belfast and three ex-Cavan.

GNR(I) Class AL 0-6-0 No 59 on Clones turntable in 1951. The 12-road roundhouse, built in the 1920s, was a twin of the one at Portadown. The cost of these two modern (for their time) structures was met from the compensation monies paid by the British government when the Great Northern, along with all the other Irish railways, was released from state control after World War One.

A Donaldson, courtesy JD Fitzgerald

Second series UG 0-6-0 No 148 of the GNR(I) heading a down 'Bundoran Express' out of Clones in early post World War Two days. The van and the first five coaches have come from Dublin via Dundalk; the final vehicle, which has come from Belfast via Monaghan, has just been attached to this train. UGs were not very often seen on the 'Express', whose normal motive power was provided by U class 4-4-0s of either the '196' or the '201' series.

JD Fitzgerald

The balance working to Belfast started from Clones. Certain of the trains were 'mixed as required' between Cavan and Clones. The commonest make-up of Cavan trains was two thirds, a first/second compo and a large van, but sometime a tri-compo replaced the first/second. More often than not, one or two small vans and/or some fitted cattle wagons would also be conveyed.

Belfast–Cavan through trains normally included tea cars in their make-up. A train composed of two K14 thirds (one a tea car), a tri-compo and a van, although common enough on this particular route, was unusual on the Great Northern as a whole, in that all seats, except those in the four-section third class end of the tri-compo, were in side-corridor compartments. On the other hand, a train with two of the older type of third class coach and an old clerestory first/second compo would be centre-corridor throughout.

During the time that the summer timetable was in force, the second morning train from Belfast included a through brake tri-compo for Bundoran. This vehicle came off at Clones where it joined two other coaches (another brake tri-compo and a tea car third) which had left Dublin on the 09.00 and had come forward from Dundalk on the 10.12 to Enniskillen. The three Bundoran coaches were taken on to Bundoran ahead of the regular Enniskillen train by a Clones engine. Stops were made at Enniskillen, Pettigo, Belleek and Ballyshannon only. The return workings of these carriages were by the same Clones engine to Bundoran Junction, from where the Dublin vehicles went forward to Dundalk by the Derry–Dundalk 'Irish North' connection into the up Mail.

Meanwhile the Clones loco took the Belfast coach to Omagh, where it was attached to the 16.10 Mail ex-Derry. The Clones engine finally got back to its home shed at the head of an 'all stations' Omagh to Clones train, which for the duration of the summer timetable took the place of an Omagh to Enniskillen railcar

service as far as the latter town. The workings which have just been described were the forerunners of the 'Bundoran Express' of the 1940s and 1950s.

Although not directly relevant to Belfast–Cavan services, a comment regarding the Dublin–Bundoran through carriages may be of interest. The addition of these two vehicles to the up Mail at Dundalk brought the standard summer load of this train up to nine bogies for the second half of its journey, about the limit for a rebuilt S class 4-4-0. The schedules then in force were 25 minutes for the 22½ miles to Drogheda, including the adverse gradient up to Hainestown on leaving Dundalk, and the climb up to Kellystown summit; and 34 minutes for the 31¼ miles from Drogheda to Dublin. With the tight connection into the evening mail steamer from Dun Laoghaire Pier, time was kept except under the most adverse circumstances. Eighty miles per hour down Rush bank was common, and although this speed may not quite have been reached down the south side of Kellystown (after all, there was the interlaced track over the Boyne viaduct and the sharp curve through Drogheda at the foot of the bank), speeds in the high 70s were certainly the norm before steam was shut off and the first brake application made after passing the warning hooter just to the north of the cement factory junction.

However, the descent of Kellystown by up trains (on the down side it was a different matter) was not much more than a dawdle by top mainline standards of the 1930s. Speeds of over 90 mph have been recorded on the up Mail coming down the Wellington bank towards Dundalk. One day, many years after the period under consideration, I was discussing the S class engines with the late Harry Wilson, the last Great Northern Mechanical Engineer: He commented, "When the S class came down the Wellington bank, you just about saw the daylight under the wheels."

Goods Services

So much for passenger trains and their workings. When I turn my mind back to the operation of mainline goods services, two points are prominent. The first of these is that since most of the trains ran at night I saw very little of them and hence can say correspondingly little about them. All through services from Belfast to Derry, to Enniskillen via Omagh, and to Clones come into this category. The mainline goods workings with which I was most familiar were the 'Porter train' (a nickname for Guinness), Dundalk–Portadown trains seen at Goraghwood, and the numerous livestock specials.

My second point concerns locomotives. During the decade of the 1930s the Great Northern acquired what, in relation to its overall total of about 200 engines, was a fair number of new passenger and 'mixed traffic' locos. There were the last five of the 4-4-2Ts in 1930, the five 'Compound' 4-4-0s in 1932, and the five UG 0-6-0s in 1937–38. As well as these 15 completely new machines, the five S and three S2 4-4-0s were heavily rebuilt in 1938 and 1939, making them the virtual equivalent of new engines. In this respect it is interesting to note that on their reappearance in traffic all of these eight engines carried plates lettered 'Built Dundalk', and the appropriate date, rather than 'Rebuilt'.

By comparison with the spate of building of 4-4-0s, tank engines and mixed traffic 0-6-0s, no new specifically goods engines had been built since 1924, when the last five SG2 0-6-0s were delivered. These indeed turned out to be the last goods engines acquired by the Great Northern.

What locomotives, then, were available to work mainline goods trains in the last inter-war decade? First, there were the SG3 0-6-0s, (generally known as the 'Big Ds'). The 15 engines of this class were built by Beyer Peacock in 1920–21 and not only marked the culmination of the steady development of the

0-6-0 type on the GNR(I) since the 1880s, but were the largest and heaviest 0-6-0s ever to run in Ireland. The SG3 was as good an example of a basic Stephenson traditional goods engine as could be found anywhere in Ireland or Britain, and was well liked by both footplate and shed staffs. Footplate staff appreciated its good steaming properties and ample reserves of power – a 'Big D' was always good for two or three more than the scheduled maximum number of wagons on the Wellington or Pomeroy banks). Shed staff liked the simple 'no frills' construction which produced few headaches in maintenance work.

The 'Big Ds' worked all over the main line, on Portadown–Dublin as well as Belfast–Derry trains and other turns. However, my most lasting memory of SG3s in the 1930s relates not to any main line through working, but to the sight of one of these impressive machines bringing up the afternoon 'transfer' from the GSR at North Wall, Dublin, to the GNR(I) goods depot at Sheriff Street. This transfer was always a heavy train, as it conveyed the numerous covered wagons (including usually some of the specially built bogie type), loaded with the products of Guinness's brewery consigned to northern and north-western destinations. The long train would come slowly up the bank round the Drogheda curve, on to the main line at East Wall Junction and then propel back into Sheriff Street, from where, not long afterwards, the afternoon down goods, the 'Porter train', would emerge at the start of its journey to Portadown. At the latter station the train would be broken and its wagons remarshalled into trains for Belfast and Derry directions. The normal working was for the 'Porter train' to leave Dublin soon after the departure of the 15.15 down express.

The SG3s, with their 5'0" diameter boilers, 19½" x 26" cylinders, 8" piston valves and 5'1" wheels, were a direct development of the SG and SG2 types which dated from 1913 and 1915 respectively. These latter engines were

SG2 0-6-0 locomotive No 18 of the GNR(I) approaching Navan Junction on the Oldcastle line. The tracks diverging to the left beyond the cabin are part of the former Midland Great Western/Great Southern (and finally CIÉ) lines from Clonsilla on the Dublin–Galway main line, to Kingscourt. Gypsum mines at the latter town provided regular transfer traffic to the GNR(I) at Navan Junction for onward transit to Drogheda cement works. There was also cattle traffic from the Kingscourt line to Belfast via Navan.

A Donaldson, courtesy JD Fitzgerald

the goods versions of the S and S2 4-4-0s. The boilers, grate areas, cylinders, valves and valve motions were identical for both the six- and the four-coupled locos. For example, the SGs had the rocker-actuated Stephenson valve gear of the S class, whilst the SG2s, like the S2s, had direct motion, as had the SG3s.

Although there was a general belief on the Northern that a 'Big D' had been timed at a speed of over 60 mph, the class was not as free running as the SG or SG2, and, while the engines of the two latter classes were often used on excursion and suburban trains, it was uncommon to see a 'Big D' on passenger work. I can remember only two occasions; once when one of these locomotives plus a single coach substituted for a railcar between Derry and Omagh, and the second time when the engine of the 08.15 Belfast–Dublin express failed at

Drogheda and an SG3 took the train on to Dublin.

In common with all Great Northern 0-6-0s, except the UGs, the SG3s had lever reverse, very handy for shunting and pick-up goods work, but requiring plenty of brute strength to adjust cut off when running.

There was another class of heavy 0-6-0 on the Great Northern which was also often referred to as a 'Big D', namely the LQG class. There were eventually 14 of these machines which, in their original unsuperheated form, dated from 1908. By the 1930s, however, they had all been rebuilt with superheaters and piston valves. These engines were slightly smaller than the SG3s, having 4'9" boilers and 4'7" wheels. This latter feature gave them a higher theoretical tractive effort than the larger machines, even though their cylinders had the standard 19" diameter of those of the S, S2, SG and SG2 locos, and not the 19½" of the SG3s. For what it was worth, the LQGs had the highest tractive effort of any class of Irish locomotive other than the GSR B1as (the 800 class) and the K1 2-6-0s, (the small-wheeled 'Woolwichs').

When built, the LQGs were rated at power Class 'C', but the rebuilding made them, at least nominally, the equals of the 1920–21 locos, hence their later 'D' classification and the 'Big D' nickname. Despite their power and their having a similar type of rocker-actuated valve gear to that of the S and SG classes, the LQGs were never as well liked as the SG, SG2 or SG3 engines. They were reputed not to be free runners, and to the extent that this was true (and I have no personal evidence either way, never having travelled on one of these engines) their relatively small wheels were

probably the cause. Not that small wheels per se necessarily inhibit reasonable speeds being attained, but obviously the greater the number of revolutions (piston strokes) needed for any given speed, the greater the need for ample inlet and (even more) exhaust valve arrangements. Eight inch piston valves were just about satisfactory for the S and SG classes, though here one remembers the 9" valves of the NCC 'Moguls' and 'Jeeps' which also had 19"x 26" cylinders. For wheels of less than 5'0" diameter, something larger would seem to have been needed for even moderately fast running. However, since the LQGs spent virtually all of their lives on loose-coupled goods trains the above speculation is largely academic.

The SGs, SG2s, SG3s and LQGs provided the motive power for most of the goods trains seen on the main line. The heavy goods loco category should possibly also include the

Class SG3 0-6-0 (a 'Big D') No 7 of the GNR(I) on an up goods at Monaghan. Note the cattle wagons – livestock formed a very significant proportion of the traffic on the Portadown–Clones–Cavan line. The presence of an AEC railcar set at the down platform dates this picture to 1950 or later. Note the 'middle road', a feature of several Great Northern passenger stations, for example Drogheda, Enniskillen, and Ballyhaise.

WT Scott

GNR(I) Class NQG 0-6-0 No 38 stopped at the Cement Factory Junction, Drogheda. The NQGs, though relatively small engines, had a high tractive effort and so were well suited to head the heavy cement trains over the short but steeply graded line from the factory to the main line. From the time when factory and siding came into use in 1936 until the end of steam on CIÉ early in 1963, one or two NQGs were always to be seen at Drogheda. The overhead cableway in the background conveyed limestone from a nearby quarry to the factory.

AE Bennett, JD Fitzgerald collection

NQGs which were a smaller (4'6") boilered version of the LQGs, and which, like them, had been rebuilt with superheaters and piston valves. I have no clear pre-war memories of these engines (one of which, No 9, was towards the end of her days given an LQG boiler and reclassified accordingly), nor do I remember any engineman having much to say about them. Possibly the disappointing results from the fitting of a Phoenix superheater to No 39 in her early days affected the reputation of them all. However, genuine heavy goods or not, these engines were in power class 'C', along with the SGs and SG2s. For the record, the other members of this four engine class were Nos 38 and 112.

The 0-6-0 locomotives of power categories 'C' and 'D' were allowed to take up to 'equal to 65' over all level and reasonably graded sections of the lines, over which their weight permitted them to operate. This maximum, equivalent to 650 tons behind the tender, was governed as much by the stopping powers of brake vans as by the maximum theoretical power of the engines. The heaviest goods brake vans on the GNR(I) were the six-wheeled 25 ton vehicles, three of which somewhat surprisingly were built in Belgium in 1924. Maximum permitted loads on the Wellington and Pomeroy banks were 55 and 49 respectively for a 'D', and 48 and 39 for a 'C'. Here again, for descending trains the brake power available to the guard was a vital factor.

I cannot remember having seen a goods train being banked from Dungannon to Pomeroy, but banking of down goods trains out of Dundalk was common. The banker usually went through to Goraghwood, in which case it was hooked on behind the van, so as to provide extra brake power down the north side of the bank. This was particularly important since Goraghwood station was actually on the incline. Working a heavy loose-coupled goods train down the north side of the Wellington bank called for skillful coordination between the men on the train engine (on which the tender hand brake was the fireman's responsibility and the engine vacuum brake the driver's), the guard and the men on the banker. With such a combination there was ample stopping power, but a sudden brake application at the rear end could easily cause a breakaway which, if it occurred just in front of the van, could mean that the train might get out of control. In those cases where the banking engine was not attached to the back of the train it would come off at Adavoyle, from whence it returned to Dundalk. Although Adavoyle, with its cabin incorporated in the upper floor of the station building, was closed to traffic in 1932 or 1933, it remained a block post for many years after that date.

Special Passenger Traffic

Interesting workings involving 'C' and 'D' goods engines were the weekend transfers of empty carriages between Belfast and Dublin during the summer. On Saturdays at that time of year, and particularly during June and July, there was a heavy demand north of the border for coaches for the numerous Sunday School, Orange Order and other excursions. Conversely, if the weather was in any way reasonable, Sundays always saw heavy traffic between Dublin and the seaside resorts of Sutton, Howth, Malahide, Skerries, Balbriggan, Gormanstown and Laytown. (Mosney was a post-World War Two station), with a corresponding demand for more carriages than were normally available at Dublin and Drogheda.

Hence provision was made in the supplementary appendices to the working timetables (though not for some reason in the regular WTTs) for 12- and 14-coach trains of bogie vehicles to be worked on Saturday and Sunday nights to Dublin from Belfast or Portadown, to be returned 24 hours later. Although all GNR(I) locomotives were vacuum fitted, these empty carriage specials were provided with goods brake vans and were run at goods train speeds without the vacuum brakes being in operation.

Many years after the time I am now speaking of, Adelaide driver Arthur Boreland told me how he used to enjoy working on these specials, particularly recalling the beauty of the summer sunrise over the sea between Laytown and Skerries. I am sure that Arthur, who has long since departed to that better place where all the coal is good and all the engines steam freely, would not mind my suggesting that, as a man who enjoyed his pint, the easier Sunday availability of his favourite beverage in Dublin than in Belfast may have been an additional factor in his nostalgic recollections of the carriage specials.

Mention of Orange Order specials reminds me that at the peak of the July demand for coaching stock the GNR(I) used to hire vehicles from its southern colleague, with the result that ex-Midland Great Western six-wheelers could be seen in Enniskillen and Warrenpoint, and old GSWR bogies in Belfast. Presumably any Orangemen who were sufficiently knowledgeable about railways to realise the origin of the vehicles they were travelling in allowed their railway interest to triumph over their political convictions on such occasions. Even the DNGR was sometimes pressed into service and contributed its quota of LNWR liveried six-wheelers at such times.

As well as working the empty carriage trains, as a change from their normal duties the heavy 0-6-0s were sometimes used as GAA specials on Sundays. At times when a team from a county served by the Great Northern appeared in an all-Ireland hurling or football final, 'Cs' and even occasionally 'Big Ds' would bring into Dublin long trains of supporters who might, if traffic was exceptionally heavy, find themselves detraining at Sheriff Street goods station instead of at the neighbouring Amiens Street passenger terminus. I remember that in 1939 (I think), when Antrim were playing in a final, Sheriff Street was very much in evidence as a relief station, even to the extent of specially printed direction notices – 'To Sheriff Street Station' – being stuck up outside the entrances to the GNR(I) and GSR stations at Amiens Street.

It was not only GAA enthusiasts who required special trains to sporting fixtures. Until about 1950, rugby internationals were played in Belfast as well as in Dublin and hence there was a two-way service of mainline specials during the early part of each year. Typically, in a year when Ireland played say Wales in Belfast and England in Dublin, there would be an 'all-in' and one or two specials from Dublin to Belfast for the Welsh match, and the same provision of trains in the reverse direction for the English. In the case of the Belfast match, there could be a special from Cork as well.

Until 1941 the Great Northern had no kitchen cars, and so the pre-World War Two 'all-in' trains were made up of several dining cars interspersed with first and second class saloons and ordinary centre-corridor vehicles. These trains, on which lunch was served on the outward journey and dinner on the return, were advertised as being all first class. The only first class treatment provided for those passengers who travelled in the second class accommodation consisted of antimacassars on the tops of the seat backs. During the war years the Northern frequently made use of this ploy, and at the same time placed 'First' stickers over the 'Second' inscriptions on the carriage doors. I cannot remember if this latter subterfuge was used in the case of the 'all-ins'. Other than these 'all-in' trains, all rugby specials were composed of ordinary third class stock.

My clearest memory of a rugby special in the 1930s is of a Cork train which I saw entering the loop line side (the present Platform 5) of Amiens Street, on its return from Belfast. This was in the spring of 1939, but of the train itself, other than the obvious fact that it was composed of GSR stock, my only recollection is that it included a Pullman, one of my 'old friends' from the early days at Mullingar. The motive power, however, has remained clearly in my mind – two Q 4-4-0s, most unusual visitors to Dublin in those days. Another small point, still remembered, is that the driver of the leading engine was obviously not familiar with the loop line side of Amiens Street, as I heard him asking a GSR man on the platform about the procedure for running round his train and getting across to the Great Northern shed. It seems strange that I do not remember anything about the Southern engine that took the train on to Cork. Was I so enthralled by the exotic sight of the two Qs, one of which was complete with net apparatus for staff exchange on the Derry Road, that I omitted to look for whatever had come around from Inchicore? It seems that I must have been. Likely motive power for the second stage of the special's journey would have been a 400 or 500 4-6-0, a 'Woolwich' or a pair of large 4-4-0s. Any of these would have been such a contrast to the ex-DSER tanks, 670s and J15s, which were the usual fare served up to train watchers on the loop line platforms, that they would have stuck in my mind.

Shunting Engines

One further aspect of Great Northern mainline operations remains to be noted – the shunting engines likely to be observed in the course of a journey from Dublin to Belfast. Note that I have deliberately used the phrase shunting engine – the Great Southern employed 'pilots', the Great Northern 'shunting engines'. The only officially

Rebuilt Great Northern Railway (Ireland) S class 4-4-0 No 172, Slieve Donard, *as station pilot ('stand pilot'), at Dundalk Junction. The 2,500-gallon tender (non standard for the class as rebuilt) had been provided to enable this engine to use the short turntable at Warrenpoint. The 'stand pilot' was popularly known as the 'Ruck engine,' a designation whose origins are lost in the mists of time.*

J Kennedy

designated 'pilot' on the latter railway was the 'Stand Pilot' at Dundalk, which was never so referred to in practice but was known to all and sundry, from Dublin to Belfast and Greenore to Enniskillen, as the 'ruck engine', though what the derivation of that ugly expression was I never discovered.

Shunting in the passenger station at Amiens Street was virtually always carried out by one of the standard 4-4-2Ts, and such locos might also work transfer trains to and from the GSR goods complex at North Wall, via the Drogheda curve. As we have seen, however, a heavy transfer from GS to GNR(I) could involve the use of an SG3. My recollection is that QGT 0-6-2T No 99 was the regular shunting engine at Sheriff Street goods yard in the last few years before the war, as she

certainly was during the war years and subsequently almost to the end of the steam era. Readers who remember this engine in the 1950s will recall that she then had an extended bunker. This was not fitted until the mid-1940s, the reason being to provide sufficient capacity to hold a reasonable amount of turf briquettes.

At Drogheda two shunting engines could often be seen at busy periods, one at each end of the station. These were normally small 0-6-0s – ALs, PGs or QGs – which would also be used on the Oldcastle and Ardee branches (though I think that the last mentioned type was too heavy to work to Ardee). A regular evening duty for the engine at the south end of the station was to attach to the rear of the 18.40 express ex-Dublin the 20-ton P van for

95

The south end of Drogheda station: Oldcastle branch, sidings, and south goods yard to the left; main lines and 'middle road' to the right. A small 0-6-0 is shunting in the south yard.

Duffner, courtesy JD Fitzgerald

Strabane, which had worked down on the 17.30 local from Amiens Street. The normal culmination of this particular shunting exercise was for the engine, after it had been uncoupled from the van, to remain against the tail of the train to bank it out of the station as far as the 'limit of shunt' sign on the north side of the Boyne viaduct. Since, as we have seen, on an evening in summer when the special tourist vehicles were included in the make-up of the express, the size of this train leaving Drogheda could be ten bogies plus the loaded van. Such assistance, in view of the tight curve at Drogheda station, was very welcome, even though the train engine was a 'Compound'.

There were always several engines visible on shunting duties at Dundalk. Often the first to be seen by a passenger in a northbound train was 0-6-0T No 31, the 'crane tank' or 'works shunting engine' to give it its more formal designation. This unusual looking but extremely useful machine, which was built by

Hawthorn, Leslie in 1928, had for the first four years of its existence the distinction of being the only Great Northern locomotive with outside cylinders, and for 20 years it was the only one on which outside Walschaert's valve gear was employed.

The regular shunting engine at Dundalk Junction was No 195, a 4-4-0T, and the last surviving locomotive of the erstwhile Belfast Central Railway. This machine and the 'ruck engine' – the latter usually an S class 4-4-0 – were almost invariably present at the time of arrival of all up and down expresses. Outside of these periods, No 195 continued to carry out its not particularly onerous duties, but the 'ruck engine' would normally be found behind the shed, awaiting the arrival of the next express. The principal reason for the daily steaming and manning of this loco was to ensure that engine power was immediately available in the event of failure of the engine of an express, or of a loco about to take out a train on the 'Irish North'. The ruck engine was also available as a pilot or a banker for heavy north-going trains, either passenger or goods. Despite these occasional duties, the most usual task which I remember seeing the 'stand pilot' carrying out was transporting relieving and relieved sets of footplate men between the train engines of through mainline expresses and the shed. It was customary for the 'ruck engine' to be turned several times daily, so that as far as possible it was always facing in the correct direction for replacing the engine of any particular train.

As well as the three regulars (the crane tank, the Junction shunter and the ruck engine), the engines of Irish North and Greenore trains were often to be observed. The former were engaged in attaching or detaching Dublin–Enniskillen through coaches to and from mainline trains, while the latter, which had to propel their short trains of six-wheelers in each direction between the passenger station and Dundalk West Junction, carried out the necessary movements between arrival and departure from and to Greenore. Either GNR(I) Class JT 2-4-2Ts or DNGR 0-6-0STs were used on the passenger and mixed trains between Greenore, Dundalk and Newry. Mixed trains were never seen at Dundalk Junction – goods and cattle wagons on the back of passenger trains ran to and from Dundalk (Barrack Street) only.

GNR(I) JT class 2-4-2T No 95 at Belturbet, the terminus of the 4¾ mile branch from Ballyhaise on the Clones–Cavan line. The date is May 1950. The six JTs, built between 1895 and 1902, worked on the Dublin suburban services until 1921, after which they were dispersed to various country branches. One shunted at Great Victoria Street, Belfast, while some worked on the Dundalk, Newry and Greenore lines from 1933 until the closure of 1950, after which scrapping commenced. No 93 went to the Belfast Transport Museum whilst No 91 remained on the Belturbet branch until this closed in 1959. This loco went to CIÉ on the break-up of the Great Northern, and lasted until the end of steam there in 1963. Note the high-sided loco coal wagon and the standard wagon loaded with sugar beet.

JD Fitzgerald collection

GNR(I) Class JT 2-4-2T No 90 on a Belturbet branch train at Ballyhaise. The stationmaster's house in the background is one of the standard GNR(I) design to be seen all over the system, and several of which are still extant today, some as private houses. Note also the typical GNR(I) building for minor country stations on the far platform.
L Hyland

Journeying northwards beyond Dundalk, our late 1930s travellers might get a glimpse, as their train left Goraghwood, of a small 0-6-0 from Newry shed shunting in the ballast quarry sidings, but they would have to continue on to Portadown before they could be sure of seeing further shunting activity. At this important junction they would have been very unlucky had they not been able to observe yet another small six-coupled tender engine at work (or possibly gently simmering while the crew downed their sandwiches and the contents of the black can) in the goods yard on the south-east side of the line, immediately to the east of the junction. At the passenger station there were shunting movements at certain times of the day, concerned with the Dublin–Derry through coaches and the numerous four- and six-wheeled vans which were such common adjuncts to the tails of Derry and Cavan trains. Passenger shunting at Portadown was normally carried out by 4-4-2Ts between their duties on Belfast trains.

About a mile on the Dublin side of Great Victoria Street terminus, Belfast, were Adelaide shed, marshalling yard, wagon shop and stores, and here there were always shunting movements in progress to interest our hypothetical travellers, provided that they could divert their gaze from the locomotives of all types standing outside the shed. There were shunting rosters for loco coal, wagon shop and stores as well as for the marshalling yard, and on these duties one saw 0-6-2Ts and 0-6-4Ts of Classes QGT and RT respectively, as well as the ubiquitous A, AL and PG small 0-6-0s. If one was particularly lucky, one might see one of the oldest GNR(I) 0-6-0s, dating from the early 1870s and originating from the Irish North Western and Ulster Railways. So far as I recall there were about four of these old machines still extant in 1938.

This has to be the author's favourite GNR(I) picture. Three-cylinder Class V 4-4-0 No 85, Merlin, heading the up Dublin Mail out of Belfast in June 1932, not long after it and its four sisters had been delivered by Beyer Peacock. Note the lined black livery, 3,500-gallon tender 'stolen' from a 'Big D' 0-6-0, and the high standard of cleanliness. Note also the original boiler with round-topped firebox. Merlin, which has been preserved by the Railway Preservation Society of Ireland, is now in the blue livery introduced in 1936, and has a Belpaire boiler. The loco is a well known performer on steam specials on the lines of both Northern Ireland Railways and Iarnrod Eireann. W Robb

Ex-Belfast and Northern Counties Railway 0-6-0 No 19 shunting at Belfast during LMS/NCC days. The tender looks quite appropriate for the locomotive, in contrast to the impression created by similarly ancient vehicles attached to some of the relatively modern U2 4-4-0s. W Robb

Rebuilt GNR(I) Class PPs No 44 heading a return Bangor excursion just to the west of the 'rickety bridge' over the River Lagan on the Belfast Central line. The lines diverging to the left gave access to Donegall Quay (identified by the cranes in the right background) and the harbour tramway. The signal man stands ready to take the staff controlling the single line from Ballymacarrett Junction. The rake of open wagons may well have brought in sand to Maysfield goods yard from Coalisland on the Cookstown branch, and could be awaiting an outward loading of coal from Queens Quay on the opposite side of the river, reached via Ballymacarrett Junction.

A Donaldson, courtesy WT Scott

The large goods yard at Grosvenor Road, Belfast, which was situated alongside the passenger station, was awkwardly placed for the observation of locos by persons in passing trains, but occasionally one might see an RT or a QGT at work. At the terminus, as in Dublin and Portadown, the shunting of passenger stock was mostly performed by 4-4-2Ts.

Shunting and transfer duties were constant activities on the Central Line, which left the main line at Central Junction; at Maysfields goods and cattle depot; and on the dock lines on either side of the River Lagan.

The smaller rail-connected areas of the Dublin docks had been known to me since about 1930. My chief recollections of the early days are of the capstans and wire ropes used to propel wagons of perishable traffic between the LMS (formerly LNWR) yard at North Wall and the Holyhead cargo steamer berths, and to

provide motive power to get the short all-steel ex-MGWR loco coal wagons to and from the quayside near the Point Depot. Before the 1925 amalgamation, these wagons would probably have been loaded at the Royal Canal Dock.

The GSR in the late 1930s

I have said a fair amount about the Great Northern during the last few years of the 1930s, but unfortunately I cannot be anything like as comprehensive about the Great Southern during the same period. Apart from two short but well remembered journeys, and some train watching from No 5 platform at Amiens Street, occasional trips to Bray represented the sum total of my GSR involvement during 1937–39.

The first of the two journeys more or less paralleled a Great Northern activity which had

A return Bangor excursion near Central Junction, Belfast, headed by Ulster Transport Authority Class UG 0-6-0 No 47 (formerly GNR(I) No 82 of the 1937 series). Note the 2,500-gallon tender of the type introduced on the 1947 UGs. Note also the letters 'UT' stencilled on the end of the leading coach. Just before the break-up of the Northern, all locos and rolling stock were thus branded 'UT' and 'CIÉ,' according to which of the predators the particular pieces of the corpse had been allotted.

JD Fitzgerald

Rebuilt GSWR/GSR 321, later D2, class 4-4-0 No 328 piloted by rebuilt 60 (D14) class No 95 leaving Kingsbridge (now Heuston) in the late 1940s, at the head of a Dublin–Limerick train. The leading vehicle is one of the 66'0" twelve-wheelers built for the Cork–Rosslare boat trains in 1907.

J Kennedy

a considerable appeal to me, namely to travel to Drogheda on the 18.40 express and return on the up Mail. My comparable exercise on the GSR was to take a return ticket from the then Kingsbridge to Kildare, going down by a late afternoon train and returning by the up Limerick (complete with Pullman). I am afraid that details of the down journey have been mostly forgotten, but on the up one, in which I travelled in the Pullman, I can recall a spirited descent of the Curragh bank. I also remember the impressive appearance of the rebuilt Class 321 loco, so clean that even the nondescript grey and black paint, with which Inchicore bedaubed its engines, looked presentable.

My second journey was by a Sunday 'mystery train' which ended up in Tullamore. I travelled in an ex-GSWR eight-compartment side corridor third and was fascinated by the row of doors all along the corridor, accustomed as I was to the centre corridors of the Great Northern thirds and the sliding doors of the Scottish vehicles. Altogether I had a feeling of being in foreign parts, which was enhanced when, in the course of a walk along the canal bank in Tullamore, I beheld a man riding a genuine 'penny farthing' bicycle. Over 40 years later I kept a small cabin cruiser on this same canal, and in the 1980s passed through Tullamore several times en route to and from the River Shannon. The only bicycles encountered on these occasions were conventional ones at the bottom of a lock, deposited by some antisocial vandal or vandals.

As regards my observations on the South Eastern line, there were certainly improvements to be seen since my Shankill days. The '670' class 0-6-2Ts were much in evidence, though whether they were as great an improvement on the DSER 4-4-2Ts and 2-4-2Ts, as the new steel-panelled suburban coaches were on the still all-too-common six-wheelers, is a debatable point. I have three specific memories of these latter extremely comfortable vehicles. First, they had particularly good seats in the third class; second, they were exceptionally spacious – too spacious, indeed, to be economical for commuter trains; and third, they always had a peculiar smell, possibly emanating from the rubber interiors of the seat cushions. Analogous to this point, older GNR(I) coaches often smelt strongly of disinfectant, not unpleasant but distinctive. All of which recollection of smells reminds me that my good friend Willy Sefton, one-time Chief Clerk in the Great Northern operating department, maintained that the sandwiches in the tea cars tasted of paraffin oil. Willy was a GNR(I) man of many years experience when I knew him, and so presumably knew what he was talking about. For my part, however, either I was lucky or I had a different sense of taste to his.

To return to the new Great Southern suburban stock, despite the attraction of these vehicles only a few of them were built and plenty of six-wheelers remained on both the coast and Harcourt Street lines. Irrespective of their 100-seat thirds, the Great Northern at least had all-bogie trains. The six-wheelers were used in the Dun Laoghaire Pier trains as well as between Dublin, Bray and Greystones. At a time when new LMS stock was becoming increasingly available for the 'Irish Mail' and other trains to and from Holyhead, these antedeluvian Irish relics scarcely provided a welcome introduction to Irish railway services for first-time visitors. For the railway enthusiast, however, the Pier train, often composed of Midland Great Western six-wheelers and Great Southern and Western low-roofed short non-corridor bogies, and sometimes headed by a 2-4-0T, must have been full of interest.

A final note with regard to the late pre-war Great Southern. Although the first two articulated Drumm battery railcars were operating during the time I have just mentioned, it was only in the 1940s that I became familiar with these cars.

Part Two: The War Years and After

6 Great Southern and Great Northern

For much of the 1940–45 period I was living and working in either Dublin or Bray. Towards the end of that time, I moved to Rostrevor in County Down and became involved in work throughout Northern Ireland, also travelling regularly to Dublin. Yet again, the majority of my memories concern the Great Northern. First of all, however, an interesting GSR journey must be recalled.

In the spring of 1940, my wife and I spent a holiday on Valentia Island. Our outward trip was not particularly remarkable – we travelled by that all embracing train, the 09.30 ex-Kingsbridge, which stopped at most stations from Kildare forward, and by means of through coaches (for example to Athlone), and connections, served almost every station on the erstwhile GSWR. The 09.30 train locomotive was a 400 class 4-6-0. After changing at Mallow and again at Farranfore, we finished by travelling the length of the Valentia Harbour branch in a four-wheeled brake third, forming part of the otherwise all six-wheeled branch train behind a rebuilt J15. My memory is quite clear about travelling in the four-wheeler, the only time I have ever done so in Ireland, but whether I was able to establish the origin of this vehicle I cannot remember now.

During our stay on the island, we made a couple of forays back to the mainland and managed some extra trips between Valentia terminus and Cahirciveen by mixed trains, invariably with J15s as motive power. It was, however, the mainline portion of our return journey to Dublin that was the highlight of our holiday travel, for not only did we come up by the Mail, resplendent with its new steel coaches and refurbished catering vehicles, but the locomotive was No 800. At that time the schedule had not been significantly altered from the 1939 figure, and there was still enough coal for it to be maintained. Hence, I remember my only run behind an 800 4-6-0 as one of my more outstanding Irish railway experiences. Possibly my most outstanding experience of all, irrespective of country, was 'footplating' on an electric locomotive over the mountain section of the Bergen–Oslo railway in Norway, but that is another story.

While waiting on the island platform at Mallow for the arrival of the Mail, I saw an obvious railway enthusiast putting on overalls, and as soon as *Maedbh* and her train arrived I observed this gentleman getting onto the engine. I must confess to experiencing a pang of envy at the stranger's good fortune. Little did I realise then, that some 30 years later I was to have many trips through Mallow on a type

A 1950s picture of Great Southern and Western 400 class (GSR Class B2a) No 402, passing Inchicore Works with a Dublin–Cork Express. Rebuilt 321 (D2) 4-4-0 No 320 stands in the siding to the right. No 402, which was reckoned to be the best of her class, together with her sisters Nos 401 and 406, was extensively rebuilt in the 1920s, receiving two 19"x 28" cylinders in place of the original four of 14"x 26". In 1937 this locomotive, at the head of a lightweight special, ran the 165½ miles from Cork to Dublin non-stop in 147 minutes.   J Kennedy

of locomotive which at the time was not merely unknown, but unimaginable in Ireland.

I have just referred to the refurbished restaurant cars in the Cork Mail set, These, Nos 2400 and 2401, were built in 1931 to the standard pattern of the wooden bogie stock of the period. No 2400 was a centre-kitchen diner with a total of 30 seats, while its companion vehicle, which accommodated 48 passengers, was designed to run with it as a trailer to provide additional accommodation for diners, and also to cater for those whose requirements were for liquid rather than solid refreshment. In 1936 these cars were rebuilt with steel side panels, to conform with the new stock for the Mail set. However, they were not as wide as the other vehicles of the train, and for the rest of their lives looked slightly incongruous when working with more modern vehicles. My recollection of No 2400 in 1940 is that, apart

from the position of its kitchen, it was very similar internally to Great Northern diner No 88, both having fixed seats of veneered wood arranged two and one on either side of the central corridor. To jump forward seven years, in 1947 No 2401 was given an end kitchen and thus became a self-contained diner, again very similar to GNR(I) No 88.

After 1940, services on the Great Southern deteriorated progressively, owing to extreme shortages of fuel and of materials for repairs and maintenance, with the result that the Dublin–Valentia return journey was the last I made over any section of the system, other than the South Eastern, for a number of years. However, during the 1942–44 period I travelled fairly regularly between Dublin and Bray by both the coastal and the inland routes. My main recollections of those days are of slow and crowded steam trains (petrol was almost

It is August 1939, and the pride of the Great Southern, the brand new 3-cylinder 4-6-0 No 800, Maedbh, has just started the heavy up day Mail from Glanmire Road station, Cork, the first GSWR or GSR loco to have done so without a pilot. Indeed, the mile-long 1:84 through the tunnel at the north end of the station, followed by the continuing heavy pull up through Rathpeacon, had on occasion needed three engines to get the Mail under way.   Cork Examiner/J Kennedy

non-existent for private cars and fuel for buses severely limited) and of the 'Drumms' on the Harcourt Street Line. There were four of these latter, each one a two-piece articulated set. The older pair generally resembled the later GSR wooden bogie stock, but with slightly rounded ends, while the later sets were steel panelled and had more pronouncedly rounded fronts and rears. The two earlier sets had originally been painted in the brown and cream of the early 1930s; subsequently they received the overall dark red livery which their younger sisters always had. Each of the four sets had both first and third class accommodation, and in each vehicle all seats were of the reversible back type, wooden framed in the older vehicles, chromium-plated metal in the later ones.

The 'Drumms' were by no means rapid movers, and their slow approach to stations,

caused by the regenerative braking, added to the overall times of journeys, but they enabled a considerably better service to be maintained on the Harcourt Street Line than would otherwise have been possible. In Bray, battery-charging facilities and a pit were provided on the down side of the running lines, just to the north of the level crossing. The siding and the pit remained in place until the 1984 electrification.

Mention of battery-charging facilities reminds me that during the war semi-underground petrol storage facilities were installed on the up side of the Bangor branch of the BCDR at Tillysburn, between Sydenham and Holywood. Apparatus for loading rail tank wagons included a number of stand pipes with bent over tops, to which flexible hoses could be attached. A Munster acquaintance of mine, on seeing these for the first time, asked were they

One of the second series Drumm electric railcars of the GSR, photographed at Inchicore Works in 1938. Note the massive batteries and the articulation of both vehicles to the centre bogie. How long would window curtains last in today's suburban trains?

J Kennedy

part of an installation for charging Drumm batteries. It may be thought that my acquaintance made a somewhat wild guess at the reason for the erection of these stand pipes, but I remember an even more far-fetched surmise. In a 1930s issue of the *Railway Magazine* there appeared a query from an English reader who, on a visit to Ireland, had seen a GNR(I) Q class 4-4-0, with the standard net arrangement for taking the staff on its tender. The query was whether the gear was for taking up mail bags. The thought of Derry Road enginemen having sufficient time to spare when negotiating the Pomeroy/Carrickmore bank, or the switchback through Annaghmore and Vernersbridge, to indulge in a little letter sorting is intriguing but scarcely realistic.

The Harcourt Street line of the GSR was not entirely a 'Drumm' preserve during the war years. A steam service, which I remember was an afternoon mixed train (I think it left Bray at 15.30), provided freight facilities for Shankill and Foxrock. This train usually included an ex-

DSER first class six-wheeled coach in its formation, a distinctive vehicle in its GSR livery, with its wide and slightly rounded profile, spoked wheels and brown velvet upholstery. My mental picture of the train shows it being headed by a '670' class 0-6-2T, but no doubt other motive power was also used. Certainly in 1944 there was at least one ex-Cork Bandon and South Coast Railway 4-6-0T working from Bray, though I recall this engine chiefly as heading an early morning up train on the Westland Row line.

For a time during the war there was some Great Northern and Great Southern through running, the Great Northern, being better off for coal than its neighbour, providing some loco workings over the DSER line. My only clear recollection of an example of through working, however, relates to Northern and not Southern metals. The sight of a standard GNR(I) 4-4-2T heading a train of ex-Midland Great Western six-wheelers, over the bridge at the eastern end of Fairview Park, was sufficiently unusual to have remained with me ever since.

Readers may well think that the temporary wartime cooperation in the running of Dublin suburban services was just a forerunner of a permanent state of affairs to come some years later, after the demise of the Great Northern. Be that as it may, I think that this is a suitable place to record a tale told to me soon after that sad event by Mr Carson, who was at the time acting as Chief Civil Engineer of the Great Northern and who transferred to CIÉ at the break up.

Soon after the change Mr Carson was provided with an office at Westland Row, headquarters of the CIÉ Civil Engineering department. Not long after he had sat down at his new desk, on the first day after his move, an elderly porter appeared carrying a bucket of coal for the office fire. "I hear you are a Great Northern man" said the bucket carrier. Mr Carson agreed that such was the case. "I am a DSE man myself" was the reply. "They're after taking you over, and now they'll ruin you the way they ruined us." The Dublin and South Eastern had been officially dead for 33 years, but not only was it still alive (if not well) and living at Westland Row, in the opinion of at least one of its erstwhile employees, but the Satanic acolytes of Kingsbridge were still in excellent health and poised to exercise their evil machinations on yet another decent railway.

As compared to the Great Southern, which had to curtail all services drastically from 1941 onwards, the Great Northern, whilst reducing its passenger services in the Irish Free State, experienced in Northern Ireland major increases in both passenger and goods traffic.

GSR, ex-Cork, Bandon and South Coast Railway, Class B4 4-6-0T No 466 on her home ground at Rocksavage, Cork. Engines of this class worked all types of train on the 'Bandon' and after the amalgamation were equally at home on the banks and curves between Dublin and Greystones, where they worked suburban passenger trains with conspicuous success. No 466, which was for a time shedded at Bray, was regarded by Inspector Bill McDonnell, a discerning judge, as "the best all rounder of her class".

J Kennedy

This led to the provision of many more trains and, coupled with increases in traffic but no extra trains in Éire, even enabled the company to pay a small dividend on its ordinary stock.

Let us now take a look at the southern section of the GNR(I) during the earlier 1940s. Coal available within Éire was no more plentiful for the Great Northern than for the Great Southern, but fortunately the GNR was able to reach agreement with the wartime Coal Controller in Northern Ireland that all locomotives operating into, as well as wholly within, Northern Ireland could be coaled there.

Since some of the most important directions of operation were Dublin–Belfast for passenger traffic, Dublin–Portadown for goods traffic, and Cavan–Clones–Portadown–Belfast and Dundalk–Enniskillen for both types of traffic, it will be realised that compared to the Great Southern, the Great Northern was able to operate reasonably comprehensive services south of the border. Mainline passenger trains became progressively heavier as the war continued, but paradoxically this tended to improve the coal situation in Éire. From 1941–42 onwards it became common for these trains to be double headed over the Wellington bank between Dundalk and Goraghwood. Usually in such cases the pilot loco of a down train after coming off at Goraghwood ran light to Newry, turned and coaled there and returned to Dundalk piloting an up train. The result was a net gain of something over four tons of coal for use in the Irish Free State. The Dundalk–Goraghwood pilots were frequently QL 4-4-0s from Amiens Street shed, which

GNR(I) S class 4-4-0 No 174, Carrantuohill, *but bereft of its nameplate, piloting S2 class No 190,* Lugnaquilla, *for which nameplates were cast in 1915 but not fitted until 1939, on a Dublin–Belfast express out of Dundalk in 1937, the year before the start of rebuilding the S and S2 engines. No 174 was rebuilt and had its nameplates restored in November 1939, whilst No 190 received the same treatment in June of that year. All eight of the rebuilds were turned out in the blue livery first used on the Class V compounds in 1936.*
Kelland Collection, courtesy JD Fitzgerald

would, in the course of a day's work, operate a 'local' Dublin–Dundalk return as well as their pilot duties. Transfer of some coal from the tenders of the QLs to the bunkers of the tank engines working on the Dublin suburban services was by no means an unknown practice, whilst the Adelaide 'Compounds' on the intercity services and the 0-6-0s on the mainline goods trains also had their tenders lightened during their lay-overs in Dublin. Drogheda, Dundalk and Clones engines were also 'importers' of coal, Clones being particularly well-situated in this respect.

I never discovered the specific arguments used by the GNR(I) management to persuade the Coal Controller to allow coaling of Éire-based engines in Northern Ireland, but such would not have been hard to find. As the war continued and food became increasingly stringently rationed in Northern Ireland, more and more Ulster people crossed the border, whilst their numbers were further increased by first rationing, and subsequently complete withdrawal, of petrol for private cars for 'pleasure' purposes. Vast numbers of cattle went north by rail to augment the scanty meat rations, and Drogheda cement works were hard put to meet the demand for cement for various aspects of wartime construction in Northern Ireland, including airfield runways. All these items – passengers, cattle and cement – had to be transported by rail, and obviously it was a case of 'no coal, no transport'.

However, despite the relatively favourable coal situation in its southern areas, the Great Northern had to curtail services there, particularly from mid-1942 onwards, at which time the 06.40 and 12.00 down mainline trains and the 14.45 and 19.10 up services were withdrawn. Seeing that the overall numbers of those travelling by rail increased greatly at the same time, the result was inevitable – much heavier trains. For the last three wartime years the basic weekday Dublin–Belfast service comprised down trains at 09.00 and at approximately 14.40 and 18.00. Up trains left Belfast at around 08.15, 12.00 and 18.00. There was also an early morning down newspaper train, of which more later. The times just quoted (except that of the 09.00 which did not alter throughout the war) were subject to change from time to time, as for instance when 'Double Summer Time' was in operation in Northern Ireland but not in the Irish Free State. This produced interesting timetable information, such as, for instance, up trains being shown to arrive at Dundalk 26 minutes before leaving Goraghwood. (Who thought that only Concorde was capable of such feats?)

Although steam trains did not disappear from either the main line or Howth branch local services, Dublin commuters relied heavily on the articulated railcars during the war years. For much of the time the last suburban buses left the city centre at about 21.30, and anyone wanting to reach the northern suburbs after that time depended on the Great Northern. In this context, the term northern suburbs is not narrowly used. In my own case, living in Dollymount and sometimes having to be late in town, I would return as far as Killester by the railcar leaving Amiens Street at about 23.00, and walk the rest of the way. Two- and three-mile walks from other suburban stations were acceptable ways of returning home. I have earlier mentioned the overloading of a triplet articulated railcar on a Belfast–Warrenpoint excursion. However, on that occasion every passenger at least had a seat, albeit perhaps on an ordinary hard, upright chair. On the wartime last train to Howth you were lucky to get a space on which to put your feet, and not to remain suspended in mid-air, supported merely by the pressure of those on either side, in front of and behind you.

To return to mainline services in the early and mid-1940s, wartime additions to the 09.00 down express were a through brake tri-compo for Derry and a customs sealed van for

Strabane for 'Free to Free' traffic, to County Donegal. In pre-war days the main Dublin–Donegal connections had been by the 06.40, 12.00 and 15.15 down trains, the last of which conveyed a through coach for Derry. Although there was a connection for Derry off the 09.00 at Portadown, this train had only limited Donegal connections at Strabane. Now, however, with only one morning down train each weekday, it was essential that reasonable Donegal connections were provided for it. In the event, there were, from 1942, two through carriages per day between Dublin and Derry, since the long-established service by the 15.15 continued to operate, though of course the departure from Dublin was somewhat altered.

The sealed van on the 09.00, which started as a brake third with its luggage accommodation sealed between Dundalk and Strabane, was an innovation. Various customs-sealed facilities for freight and parcels had been in operation for Donegal traffic before the war, and there was also provision for the passage of passengers' luggage between Britain and Northern Ireland via Holyhead and Dun Laoghaire without examination, but the Strabane sealed van was the first such provision for passengers' luggage, as well as parcels and freight, between Dublin and County Donegal. At the start of the full van service (as distinct from the brake thirds) ordinary 'M vans' of passenger vehicle type were used, but later on there was a tendency to use 20 ton capacity vacuum-fitted bogie freight vans of type P.

Readers with an aptitude for figures may have deduced from an earlier paragraph that wartime passenger trains were allowed 34 minutes from Goraghwood to Dundalk, a scarcely inspiring figure even allowing for much heavier trains than those of 1939, when the time had been 25 minutes. A partial explanation of this apparently savage deceleration, however, is that 34 minutes was the 'time shown to the public' – the working book

allowed only 29. The cause of this disparity in figures was that with both outward and inward customs examinations in each direction, coupled with security checks in Northern Ireland, there were frequently long delays at both Dundalk and Goraghwood, making it advisable to allow some recovery time.

For a while an attempt was made to reduce the delays at Dundalk by having customs examinations carried out on the trains between that station and Drogheda, in either direction. This procedure necessitated the segregation of passengers to and from Drogheda and Dublin, who joined or left the trains at Dundalk, from cross-border travellers. This was effected by marshalling one of the tri-compo bogie carriages, referred to earlier in connection with Belfast–Cavan services, at the ends of Belfast–Dublin trains between Dundalk and Dublin. Often, however, at weekends and busy holiday periods, the numbers travelling called for duplication of services south of Dundalk, in which case the Dublin to 'Irish North' coaches formed a separate train.

I have often wondered if the separate Dublin–Dundalk coaches were all that successful in reducing customs delays, for it was not just the time taken for the preventive officers to go through a train that caused the long waits. A considerable amount of time was also taken up by the interrogation and searching of suspected smugglers in the customs offices at the border stations. Obviously the searches had to be conducted in private, as it was not feasible to carry out any serious degree of interrogation in full view and hearing of a carriage full of passengers. The Great Northern announced in various public notices that trains would not be delayed for the examination of passengers' luggage. If examination could not be concluded by scheduled departure time, the train would not be delayed and the unexamined luggage would be removed "and forwarded to destination as soon as possible thereafter". In practice, however, this never happened. The customs officers, in Northern Ireland and the Irish Free State, had the final say in whether a train might depart on time or be retained for completion of examination, and they would never give the all clear until they had quite finished their antics. I understand that this was because they wished to avoid the possibility of action being taken against them by someone whose luggage had been removed from the train without anything incriminating being found.

The reduction in the number of through mainline services in 1942 was probably as much due to the extreme demands being made on locos and carriages as it was to shortage of coal. Whatever the reason, there were now only three Dublin–Belfast trains each weekday, and in most cases these were made up to what were, compared to pre-war practice, impressive lengths. The same applied to the two Sunday trains each way which now operated in place of the three of earlier days. Train loads, excluding any Derry, Enniskillen or Warrenpoint through coaches, rose from six or seven to eight, nine or ten, with the result that, taking through carriages into account, 12-bogie formations were common. The numbers of all three classes of passengers increased, but proportionately more for first and second than for third.

On the mainline expresses 'Superior class' accommodation, as it was officially designated, frequently consisted of an old brake second at the south end of the train, with two of its compartments restored to their original status as firsts, followed by two first/second compos, or a compo and an all first. In either case, one of these latter would probably be a pre-1914 clerestory vehicle. I remember one journey from Dublin to Goraghwood, on the afternoon train, when the extra vehicle was an open 'saloon carriage'. Third class, north of the catering vehicle, usually comprised four K15s and a brake third. Occasionally, the third class accommodation would be augmented by a GSR coach. There was a long-standing

regulation that passenger trains over the Wellington bank should have a brake vehicle at either end, this no doubt dating from very early pre-continuous brake days, but generally speaking it was still being adhered to in the 1940s, mostly by the provision of brake thirds and brake composites. One of the very few times that I remember seeing the regulation disregarded was when I observed an ex-GSWR full third at the very head of a Belfast train leaving Amiens Street.

Catering services were considerably affected by the increased traffic. The number of passengers requiring full meals grew to such an extent that the buffet cars were no longer suitable for use in Dublin–Belfast trains, owing to their limited kitchen facilities. They were transferred to the Derry Road, on which there were now five through trains instead of the pre-war four, each of which had a restaurant or buffet car. Heavy military traffic to and from such places as Omagh and Enniskillen no doubt swelled their receipts.

On the main line, for most of the time when only three weekday intercity trains were operating, the new (1938) restaurant car No 88 worked in the 09.00 ex-Amiens Street and in the evening up service from Belfast. In contrast to the pre-war situation, when three of the five regular sets had been Dublin based, two of the three now operating were stabled in Belfast, leaving No 88 as the sole catering vehicle based in Dublin all the year round. However, once the 'Bundoran Express' became established as a separate train, rather than a couple of through carriages, a second car worked from Dublin during the summer months. My recollection is that either No 266 or No 267 buffet car was used on this service for at least one season.

The transfer of one of the 1936 buffet cars to the 'Irish North' would still have left Belfast–Derry trains with two modern buffets, since a third such vehicle, No 124, came from Dundalk works in 1941. This new car was broadly similar to Nos 266 and 267, but differed from them in having two plus one seating for 30 instead of two plus two for 40, and in having the kitchen between the bar and the tabled accommodation instead of at one end. Another difference was that the entrance doors at the end away from the bar opened into a small vestibule and not directly into the seated accommodation. Externally, No 124 could be distinguished from its predecessors by its rather shallower windows.

The three most recently built wooden dining cars – Nos 401, 402 and 144 – each had extra seating installed, which was provided by moving the tables and chairs closer together. The reason for this was both obvious and compelling, but it resulted in the seating being out of balance with the windows, and also of course in the accommodation being cramped. One of these three cars worked in the up morning and down afternoon mainline trains, whilst a second, for a short while after the reduction in services, was in the noon up and evening down set.

Which of the three vehicles worked on which service varied. For a time No 402 was in the morning up train, No 144 in the 12.00 and No 401, formerly the mainline mail car, was on the Derry Road. Before long, however, a single car became quite inadequate to cater for the large numbers requiring lunch on the 12 noon and dinner on the evening down train.

The problem was solved by the conversion of two bogie vans, Nos 272 and 399, to kitchen cars, and the adaptation of an old second class saloon, No 407, as a first class restaurant trailer. This latter vehicle was a clerestory-roofed former restaurant car which dated from the early years of the century. Only first and second class passengers were accommodated in No 407, thirds being catered for by reserving the half of the K15 nearest the kitchen car for the service of meals. As my copy of the GNR(I) carriage list issued during the war years is now in the Irish Railway Record Society archives, I cannot check my recollection that the coach most often used as a half-dining trailer was No 77. With the new arrangements, there were 68 seats available for meal service on the 12 noon Belfast–Dublin train and its return working.

Usually, there would be three sittings for lunch. As the overall city to city times were by now all considerably over the three hours, due principally to customs delays, there was ample time for such a protracted service. In my experience, few dining car seats were ever vacant on the 12 noon up or evening down trains, which meant that a total of just over 200 lunches or dinners would be prepared, served and consumed in the course of an intercity journey. Despite the kitchen car being based in Belfast, much of the provisioning was done on the southern side of the border where food rationing was not as stringent as it was in Northern Ireland. A new, or rather rebuilt, first class restaurant trailer, No 137, seating 42 and formerly a full second, was introduced in May 1945, but despite its modern flush-sided body and two plus one seating on chairs, its old chassis and bogies made it a rough rider. It did not long survive the end of the war.

It may be thought that I have devoted an undue amount of space to wartime catering services, but this has been done deliberately, not so much on account of my own interest in a minor side of railway operation, but rather to emphasise the contrast between mainline passenger traffic and passengers' eating habits 45 years ago and at the present time.

What else do I remember about mainline passenger services during the war? So great was the demand for carriages (and military specials often called for at short notice had a bearing on availability) that non-corridor thirds were sometime included as strengtheners in the regular Dublin–Belfast sets. I saw this ploy in operation only in the evening Sunday train ex-Dublin, which was always loaded to more than capacity with weekenders returning to Belfast. The combination of full employment at good rates of pay in various aspects of war work on the one hand, and food rationing on the other, ensured that there was a steady stream of Ulster people eager to take advantage of the attractive eating and drinking facilities in the Irish Free State, and their only means of transport was the railway.

I once travelled in a non-corridor compartment third from Amiens Street to Goraghwood by that Sunday evening train. I will not go so far as to say that there was not a single seat available in a corridor vehicle, since I made a point of riding in the non-corridor, just for the experience, but certainly in the coach in which I found myself every seat was taken, and as this vehicle was at the very head of the train the chances were that there were standing passengers further back.

Although the so-called 'workmen's carriages' (Class K23) were in use in local trains in the Dublin area, as well as in Northern Ireland, I never saw one of them on intercity service. If this meant that no 'workmen's' vehicles were ever included in wartime mainline expresses, cross-border travellers had much to be thankful for. Of all the standard-gauge Irish railway coaches I ever travelled in, GNR(I) 100-seat thirds and MGWR and BCDR half partitioned six-wheelers included, the 'workmen's' coaches were by a wide margin the most uncomfortable and by far the nosiest. Outwardly these vehicles were not at all bad looking, particularly when new and before the dirt had become ingrained in the grooves between the vertical wooden panels. The coaches were built to the standard dimensions of 58'0" x 9'6", and to the profile of the latest mainline stock. Inwardly, however, they were of the most basic standard – wooden floors with no covering, low-backed wooden slatted seats on either side of a central corridor (but no corridor connections), no internal lining to the sides, and sparse 'blackout' lighting. There were four doors per side,

spaced similarly to those of the K15 mainline carriages.

Although the 'austerity' coaches were built on account of the great increase of short-distance passenger traffic in Northern Ireland, they got all over the system. Here I may recall that in contrast to the wartime passenger trains on the Great Southern, whose coaches kept their normal lighting, all Great Northern vehicles had only dim 'blackout' illumination. North of the border, station lighting too was almost non-existent. All locomotives, irrespective of what shed they were stabled at, had at all times heavy tarpaulin sheets fixed to the rear edges of the cab roofs, to be unrolled and secured to the fronts of the tenders after dark.

As well as the 'workmen's coaches', the GNR(I) managed to construct some new mainline passenger vehicles during the war. These were mainly standard open third class and side-corridor first/seconds of the types introduced in 1936, but there were also at least two side-corridor thirds (Nos 218 and 219). As built, these latter carriages had three-a-side seating with arm rests, and were used as firsts on the Bundoran express; later they reverted to their designed third class designations. As firsts they suffered badly from lack of leg room. A new buffet car, No 124, built in 1941, has already been referred to.

Increased passenger traffic was responsible for additional station facilities as well as extra coaches. In 1942 Amiens Street, Portadown and Great Victoria Street were all subject to alterations and/or additions. At Amiens Street the underground toilets were constructed, previous lavatory accommodation having been near the barrier to the present Platform No 4. The old wooden booking office in the concourse was replaced and a snack bar at the entrance to Platform No 4 was built. At Portadown a new snack bar was provided on the island platform (Nos 2 and 3), whilst at Great Victoria Street, Belfast, there was a new snack bar and also new booking office facilities in place of the old wooden structure similar to the one in Dublin. Apropos of the new toilet facilities in Dublin, I remember Harry Patterson, subsequently Chief Accountant, saying that since so many Northern Ireland people were arriving in Dublin and eating and drinking the residents out of house and home, it was only appropriate that the company should make an attempt to get something back from them. To this day, I have never been quite sure if he was referring merely to anticipated increased revenue from the paylocks on the cubicle doors.

No doubt management would have liked to improve the operating facilities (an extra cross-over at Goraghwood for example, and a modern signalling installation at Belfast), and thanks to increased traffic revenue some money would probably have been available for such work. However, materials could not be obtained, and so the greatly augmented traffic had to be dealt with within the framework of an old and inadequate track layout and old-fashioned signalling. A small amount of new track was laid during the war – a two-mile spur off the Antrim branch, strictly to government requirements – but that was about all, and in any case this did nothing to improve existing facilities. Otherwise, apart from the construction of loops at Hillsborough and Aldergrove and the adaptation of the sidings in the old quarry area at Malahide to serve as a small marshalling yard, in order to relieve pressure on the small and awkwardly laid-out 'Dublin Goods' at Sheriff Street, I can remember no improvements to running lines or sidings. There was, however, one considerable addition to operating facilities in Northern Ireland, namely the direct connection by phone of all stations in Northern Ireland with the operating office at Great Victoria Street. I understand that this installation was made at government expense.

We have seen that a prominent feature of cross-border traffic in the war years was the long delay at customs stations, up to 35 minutes in the timetables and often more in practice. At Dundalk the preventive officers were perhaps not so concerned at what might be coming in as with what Northern Ireland residents might be bringing out in the way of food, drink, clothes and shoes, all of which were strictly rationed north of the border. The sight of people being removed from down trains and subsequently returning in their stockinged feet, or looking rather thinner than when they departed, was by no means uncommon.

While awaiting the return of these unfortunates from the search chambers, any other passengers who were railway enthusiasts could pass the time by observing the movements of 4-4-0T No 195, which lasted as the Dundalk Junction shunting engine until the early post-war years. Similar customs diversions took place of course at Monaghan, Clones, Ballyshannon and elsewhere on the system, but except at Clones there would be less of railway interest to divert those lucky or clever enough to escape the attentions of the customs men.

The preventive staff at Goraghwood were alert to detect anything unlawful coming in, but, like their southern counterparts, were equally occupied in not letting goods out. I remember once in a lavatory compartment of an old standard wooden third class coach, which had a droplight window, finding a bicycle tyre stuffed down the slot into which the window descended. Being cautious, and also at that time not owning a bicycle, I left it there. An interesting minor point as regards the customs officers at Goraghwood was that several of them came originally from south of the border, being ex-members of the former Royal Irish Constabulary. At least one of them had his home outside Northern Ireland, owning a small farm near Ardee. At Goraghwood, as well as customs examinations there were security checks. All travellers were required to produce proof of identity – Northern Ireland residents at that time carried identity cards, issued to all people there and in Britain at the beginning of the war, while Irish Free State passengers required travel permits. Normally, the security men were through the train long before their customs colleagues had finished their probings and pryings.

There was an interesting example of class distinction in operation at Amiens Street during the war years. Naturally, many of the passengers who arrived by mainline trains would be looking for transport to city hotels or other destinations. Some taxis did contrive to operate throughout the war, despite stringent petrol rationing, but the supply of these vehicles was by no means equal to the demand, with the result that horse cabs and outside cars once more came into their own. Invariably drawn up along the roadway at the side of the main arrival platform (now No 2), there would be some taxis at the southern end, strategically placed for passengers in the superior class coaches, whilst behind them would be the horse-drawn vehicles.

Overall, throughout the station there was always in those days a strong smell of horse manure. On a personal note, I may mention here that the last time I travelled in, or rather on, an 'outside car' was in the year 1942 – not, however, from Amiens Street station but from Westland Row (Pearse), having arrived there in the boat train from Dun Laoghaire.

Mention of the southern end of the arrival platform at Amiens Street reminds me that double heading was not permitted there owing to weight restrictions on the bridge spanning Sheriff Street, which thoroughfare passed beneath the station. No engines at all were allowed over the final sections of the two middle roads, a state of affairs which lasted until the major alterations at Connolly during the 1980s. Readers who were familiar with the erstwhile Amiens Street may remember that above each of these middle roads (which were used for carriage storage) boards bearing the inscription "Engines must not pass this board" were hung.

What all this is leading up to is that when, during the middle war years, the up evening express from Belfast was regularly double headed (the pilot, usually a PP 4-4-0, worked down on the newspaper train), the train always stopped outside the station to detach the pilot. For some of the time during which this practice was in force I was living in Dollymount, from where, on a still evening, one could hear not only the incoming Belfast train running through Clontarf and over the Fairview Bridge, but even the pilot engine making off to the shed, followed by the sound of the 'Compound' restarting its train for the last couple of hundred yards of its journey.

Later, the working was altered so that the paper train brought up from Portadown a separate evening train composed of the through coach and the sealed van off the Derry Road, along with three or four other vehicles. This practice enabled the express from Belfast to run non-stop to Goraghwood, though, in the circumstances of the time, no great speeds were possible (the overall booked allowance for the 40¾ miles was 55 minutes).

The three or four extra vehicles on the up train from Portadown came back in the paper train and formed the 04.20 passenger to Belfast, a train which continued to be in demand for as long as many of Belfast's engineering and other factories on war work were operating for 16 or 24 hours per day. Here I should mention that after the bombing of Belfast in 1941 many people moved out of the city to live, though continuing to work in town. The result for the Great Northern was greatly increased commuter traffic from such places as Banbridge, Portadown, Armagh and Lurgan. Indeed, I knew a man who worked as a joiner in the Belfast shipyard and who lived in Rostrevor. He travelled to and from work daily, leaving Warrenpoint around 07.20, and returning on the 17.50 from Belfast. Each of these trains provided a through service between Warrenpoint and Belfast, taking about one and a half hours each way and calling at Newry (two stops – Dublin Bridge and Edward Street), Goraghwood, Poyntzpass, Scarva, Tandragee, Portadown, Lurgan and Lisburn. The single through Belfast–Warrenpoint coaches on the ends of mainline expresses were no longer adequate to cope with the traffic, now that there were several through trains, including evening services ex-Belfast at both 17.40 and 17.50.

James Lockhart, who was traffic manager of the Great Northern during the 1930s and very early 1940s, used to maintain that the Warrenpoint branch should have been capable of sustaining a separate service from and to Belfast independently of the intercity trains. Whether his opinion would have been sustainable before the war is debatable, but he was certainly vindicated from 1941 onwards.

The enhanced Warrenpoint services led to an increased allocation of locomotives to Newry shed, and to through engine workings between the branch and Belfast. Gone were the days when a couple of 4-4-2Ts coped with all the passenger work. Now, in addition to tank engines, there were three, and sometimes four, small 4-4-0s, of which I remember specifically Nos 71 and 74 and a P5'6" (number now forgotten). Nos 71 and 74 were for some time in the charge of drivers Joe Kiely and Paddy Quinn (known as 'The Bacon') respectively, and, despite wartime stringencies, were almost always spotless, even the footplate brasses being polished. Other Newry locos were also usually well turned out, and indeed Newry, with the possible exception of Drogheda, had the cleanest engines on the system during most of the 1940s.

The mainline workings by Newry engines led to some impressive feats of haulage, considering the size of the locos involved. The

08.40 ex-Warrenpoint, usually a six-bogie train, was allowed 45 minutes, with two stops, between Portadown and Belfast. This was perhaps not particularly impressive, though the likelihood of there being a tender full of indifferent coal had always to be reckoned with, but the Newry enginemen and their machine were set a harder task at the start of their journey home. The return working as far as Portadown was the 13.30 Belfast–Derry train, which might on occasion comprise up to eight coaches. The time to Portadown over a slightly harder road than in the reverse direction, and again with stops at Lisburn and Lurgan, was 45 minutes. From Portadown on to Warrenpoint the work was easier, usually with a three-bogie set, which gave the Warrenpoint connection out of the 13.30 Derry service. As regards this latter train, it is interesting to note that the old custom of changing the engines of Belfast–Derry trains at Portadown was still in force.

As evidence that it was not only on the 13.30 ex-Belfast that the small 4-4-0s from Newry shed were required to work hard, I can remember travelling from Warrenpoint to Belfast on the 18.30 to Portadown, changing at the latter station. The load was eight bogies and the engine a P5'6". The time was kept.

There was one service each way between Belfast and Warrenpoint which regularly produced an engine appreciably larger that a PP. This was the 17.40 from Great Victoria Street, which was almost invariably headed by a Q 4-4-0 from Adelaide shed. This engine and train returned to Goraghwood to provide a connection into the evening Dublin–Belfast express. The express would stand at the down mainline platform for half an hour or more, during which time the customs officers and security men plied their trade. For much of this waiting period the Warrenpoint train (now emptied of its passengers, who would be herded into the small waiting space on the down platform until the customs men had finished their work) stood on the up main line alongside the express, with their 4-4-0 engines of Classes Q and V ('Compound') side by side.

As I was travelling regularly between Dublin and Warrenpoint by the evening train from mid-1944 onward, I had ample opportunity to study the external character-istics of the Q class as I waited on the island platform (up main one side, branch the other) for my connection to Warrenpoint. My wait was appreciable since after the express had departed for Belfast, the Q and its train could not leave Goraghwood (working 'all stations' to Portadown) until the express had cleared Poyntzpass, which usually took seven or eight minutes. It was only after this down slow service had left Goraghwood that the branch train coming from Portadown (the return working of the 18.30 ex-Warrenpoint) could come in to the up main platform and subsequently proceed to Warrenpoint.

On those nights when the express was late leaving Goraghwood, resulting in a longer than usual wait for branch passengers from Dublin, Drogheda and Dundalk, one was thankful if it was Paddy Quinn's week for the late turn. The pre-war time from Newry (Dublin Bridge) to Warrenpoint had been ten minutes; now it was 12 and never in my memory did Joe Kiely urge No 71 to accomplish the six miles in anything less. With 'The Bacon' on No 74, however, there was always a sporting chance that the pre-war timing would be kept. Why such a fuss about a matter of two minutes, the reader may ask? Possibly no good reason, objectively considered, but on a winter night the impression of speed as Paddy Quinn pushed No 74 along the short rails past Aghnamoira and Narrowwater was as cheering to passengers as Joe Kiely's measured progress was dispiriting.

Even though once the branch train eventually got to Goraghwood there was nothing so far as traffic was concerned to delay it further, passengers could be subject to a further delay due to customs procedures, albeit in winter at least in usually warm coaches. The train waited until the customs officers had completed all their paper work and were ready to be conveyed down the hill to Newry, en route for home. The chief preventive officer, Mr Kearney, was an amiable man, well known to, and on good terms with, regular travellers. Nevertheless, on occasions our regard for him as a fellow citizen was sometimes more than a little strained as we sat in our static train waiting for him to appear.

This seems a suitable place to refer to the awkward track layout at Goraghwood. During all of the 1930s, all of the war years and for a considerable time thereafter this important junction, customs post and ballast depot, at which almost all trains had to stop, some of them for an appreciable length of time, had only one crossover, although there were three platform faces. The result was that any up mainline train in the station blocked both up and down branch trains from getting to and from the main line. The situation was bad enough as regards wartime passenger trains, but it was also bad when down mainline goods were in the station. Even though there was siding accommodation available, the customs officers required the trains to be at the platforms when being examined, a process that often took an hour or more.

Another by no means unimportant consequence of the absence of a second crossover, as regards down goods trains, was that if a banking engine came through from Dundalk it could not get across the road to return home until the customs had finished with the train, enabling the latter either to proceed on its journey northwards or be put into a siding. It would, of course, have been physically possible for a banking engine to have returned 'wrong line' to Bessbrook, and then rejoin the up line, but whether wrong line orders were ever issued for this purpose I do not know.

There was siding accommodation on each side of the main line at Goraghwood, in each case giving rise to difficulties in working. The down side was the easier in that although the siding was on an appreciable down gradient towards the main line, necessitating precautions that no vehicle standing there ran away, there was a straightforward set back up the hill into the siding. Matters were not so easy on the up side because, when setting back, a train first went downhill, but as soon as the actual siding was reached the gradient changed to an ascent.

The driver of an up goods shunt moving into the siding in order that a passenger train might overtake (as was frequently the case with the first morning goods from Portadown and the 08.15 passenger from Belfast), had to exercise particular care to ensure that in starting away again he steamed his engine sufficiently hard to attack the Wellington bank immediately he got back on to the main line, but at the same time not so hard as to cause a breakaway when coming out of the hole where siding and running line met.

Many years after the war I made my first footplate trip on an engine carrying out this particular manoeuvre. The loco was a 'Jeep' (an ex-NCC 2-6-4T) which, with its high wheel and relatively limited tractive effort, was not the ideal machine for working heavy goods trains over the Wellington, and which on this occasion certainly gave its driver plenty of scope to demonstrate his expertise.

While the normal line of promotion for drivers was through the goods links and the local passengers, before graduating to the express turns, and for shunters to become goods guards before they were put on regular passenger work, I always considered that in the days of loose-coupled goods trains the jobs of both drivers and guards were more arduous than those of their passenger colleagues.

I became all the more confirmed in this view in the mid-1960s after I had travelled on a B121 class 'Bo-Bo' diesel loco of CIÉ (a type generally considered to be weak in brake power) hauling a maximum weight loose-coupled through Cork–Dublin goods, the journey ending with the steep descent down through the 'Gullet' into Kingsbridge yard.

Also, as regards loose-coupled goods trains, I can recall driver Bob Perry of Portadown (known as 'The Irish Guardsman', presumably a humourous reference to his being a very small man) when I was with him on a 'Big D' working a Dundalk–Portadown goods 'Equal to 58', three over the official maximum load of '55', turning to me just after we had got to the top of the bank and saying, "Now the job is to stop them running away with you."

Before leaving the subject of wartime goods trains, some reference must be made to the livestock traffic which, in common with other sorts of freight workings, increased greatly during the early 1940s. Obviously, with meat being rationed in Northern Ireland and in Britain, there was a market for every suitable beast that could be brought over the border, with the result that not only were there down mainline cattle specials every Thursday, the day of the Dublin cattle market, but on other days of the week as well from towns in which fairs were held – prime examples being Kells and Navan. To work a stock special from Belfast to Dublin and back, empty wagons up and loaded down, required four sets of enginemen, such were the delays encountered on the heavily-used main line and in the veterinary examination of animals at Goraghwood.

In such cases footplate crews were usually changed at Dundalk in each direction. Stock specials were particularly evident north of Portadown, from where, onwards to Belfast, the Clones and Derry Roads contributed their quotas. Even places as near to Belfast as Banbridge and Lurgan provided livestock traffic, since the British Ministry of Food, which during wartime was the sole buyer of fatstock, had a regulation to the effect that, where possible, all animals travelling a distance of 20 miles or more had to go by rail. Much of the stock traffic to Belfast was for onward shipment to Britain.

Although a significant proportion of cattle and sheep traffic to Belfast, by both special and scheduled trains, originated on the Great Southern system, coming to the Northern via Navan, Cavan or Enniskillen, I do not remember having seen a Great Southern cattle wagon north of the border in the 1940s, though such vehicles from the SLNCR were common. In the case of these latter wagons, since it was not possible to provide a through one-day service from west of Ireland fairs to Belfast or Derry (from which latter port many animals were shipped to Glasgow), beasts were detrained, fed, watered and rested at Colloney and then reloaded into SLNCR vehicles for the remainder of their journeys. On a trip from say Ballinasloe to Derry via Athenry (or Athlone), Claremorris, the 'Burma Road', Enniskillen and Omagh, rest for the animals was essential.

Detraining and reloading may also have taken place at Cavan in the case of stock coming from a distance, though I understand that for cattle from Mullingar and also GSR Meath line stations via Navan, the Great Northern would sometimes provide wagons for the entire journey through to Belfast.

7 Post-War Developments, 1945–1947

Although I had made occasional journeys between Belfast and Larne and one from Belfast to Antrim in pre-war days, it was not until 1944, by which time I was living in Northern Ireland and travelling fairly extensively in the province, that I came to know the NCC railway in any detail, whilst until the same year I had had no contact at all with the BCDR. However, during the next five years I found myself well placed to observe at least some of what came and went on the NCC as well as to acquire an even closer knowledge of the Great Northern main line and Warrenpoint branch. Since the early 1930s my father had been the Rating and Valuation Consultant to all the Irish railway companies except the Belfast and Co Down, and in 1944 I started working with him preparatory to qualifying as a chartered valuation surveyor. Though my father's professional connections were with seven of the eight companies then operating, he was most closely involved with the GNR(I) and the NCC, and so I soon commenced my acquaintance with the one and extended my knowledge of the other.

During the final year of the war there was little outward change in the activities of the Great Northern. Food, petrol and clothing

LMS(NCC) 2-6-0 No 97 Earl of Ulster *at the head of the down 'Golfers' Express' at York Road station, Belfast, in 1938. This loco lasted until the end of regular steam operation (other than the 'stone trains') on the lines of the Ulster Transport Authority. No 97 ended her days working passenger trains between Belfast and Dundalk, goods trains from Portadown to Dundalk and Derry, and the occasional passenger special from Belfast to Dublin or Derry – a far cry indeed from the fliers of pre-war years*

W Robb

Belfast and County Down Railway standard tank loco No 15 on a down train at Comber in the mid-1930s. By 1949, 12 of this company's stock of 30 engines were of this class; they worked all types of trains, other than the very heaviest Bangor commuter services, all over the system.　　　　　　　　W Robb

rationing continued in Northern Ireland, and hence so did the heavy cross-border passenger and livestock traffic. Gradually however, after mid-1945, as the factories on war work closed and others slackened their activities, the intense commuter traffic into Belfast began to diminish, as did the numbers of military personnel travelling by special and ordinary trains. Coincidentally with these reductions there was an increase in the number of mainline expresses: first an early departure from Dublin with a mid-afternoon return from Belfast, and then a 10.30 from Belfast which permitted the provision of an extra evening return from Dublin. For a short while this late down train carried a through coach from Dublin to Derry.

Here are a few random recollections from the 1945–47 period.

In the summer of 1946 I made my first journey over the former Ulster Railway south of Armagh, travelling from Warrenpoint to Enniskillen. I must admit to recollecting little of this pioneer journey, save that the loco was a Q 4-4-0 and that the enginemen changed over at Tynan with the Cavan crew of a similar engine. An interesting indication of the importance of goods traffic in pre-1914 days at Glaslough, and how it had been affected by the establishment of the border, was the large double-bayed store, now partially unroofed, on the west side of the line at this small country station.

The year 1946 also saw me travelling on the BCDR for the first time, from Newcastle to Ardglass, to which small fishing port I was proceeding from Rostrevor in order to collect a boat. From Newcastle to Downpatrick I travelled in one of the relatively few bogie carriages of the 'County Down', not a particularly comfortable experience. The railway had only two recently built bogies, but I suspected that these rarely got off the Bangor branch. My train ex-Newcastle was running

Seen here is No 6, the last surviving 2-4-0 of the BCDR before its wartime rebuilding with a Belpaire boiler and a 'modernised' tender. The loco is pictured working a push pull shuttle between Comber and Glassmore during one of the Ulster TT car races in the 1930s. Note the white square on the front drawhook, turned down when the loco was propelling its train. Note also the tender cab.

W Robb

from Newcastle to Belfast via Downpatrick – it was possible to bypass the latter town via the 'loop line' – and, as I expected, was hauled by a standard 4-4-2T. I do not remember what the motive power was over the branch to Ardglass, although I do remember making my first journey in one of the notorious BCDR six-wheelers. The probable reason for my not remembering the branch locomotive is that whilst waiting at Downpatrick for my connection I was enthralled by the appearance on a down Belfast–Newcastle train of 2-4-0 No 6. This was a survivor from the nineteenth century which not only had been saved from the scrap heap but actually rebuilt as a result of the increase in traffic during the war. During the rebuilding the engine acquired a boiler of the type used on the standard tank engines, and so far as appearance went was a straightforward-looking small machine. The unusual feature about No 6 was her tender –

this was an old vehicle with the outside springs above the running plate typical of its date, but it had been given new high flush sides, resulting in an unconventional appearance.

On the Great Northern in 1946 some of the lady carriage cleaners were given brown uniforms and put to travel on through mainline trains. As well as keeping the passenger accommodation clean throughout the journey, their duties included advising passengers of impending customs examinations at Dundalk and Goraghwood. At about this time, a short-lived early morning passenger service operated from Drogheda to Goraghwood, giving a connection for Belfast. The service was provided by a railbus which, after discharging passengers at Goraghwood, proceeded to Warrenpoint from where it next ran right through to Belfast. Later still, it took itself home to Drogheda. This service did not last long since the bus was wholly inadequate to carry the traffic offering north of the border. I once travelled from Warrenpoint to Belfast in this vehicle, purely out of interest. It was not a procedure to be repeated, evoking as it did strong memories of the late evening railcar from Amiens Street to Howth of two years earlier.

In the summer of 1946 there was a bad washout of a culvert on the Derry Road between Pomeroy and Donaghmore, as a result of an exceptionally heavy rainstorm. It took about a fortnight for the damage to be repaired, during which time Goraghwood quarry was working 24 hours a day supplying material to rebuild the damaged embankment. For as long as through running was disrupted, travellers by four of the five daily passenger trains each way between Belfast and Derry, as well as by the additional Omagh–Belfast return

service, were carried by bus between Dungannon and Pomeroy. The fifth Belfast–Derry train ran via Clones and Enniskillen in each direction. (As much parcels traffic as possible was conveyed by this service in order to reduce the amount of loading and unloading at each end of the road section.) In 1946 there were still extensive catering services on the Derry trains, including the provision of a restaurant car on the 13.30 ex-Belfast, the train which ran via Clones. This diverted train, and a similar one a few years later when a second but less drastic washout occurred between Dungannon and Pomeroy, must have been one of the very few ever scheduled to convey a dining car between Clones and Omagh.

There had been tea cars at various times between Derry and Dundalk via Enniskillen,

A Drogheda-based railbus on the Oldcastle branch of the GNR(I). For several years one of these vehicles operated a daily round of two return trips between Drogheda and Navan, and one from Drogheda to Oldcastle and back. However, for a short time in the early postwar years a more ambitious railbus roster was also in place, comprising Drogheda–Warrenpoint–Belfast–Drogheda, as described in the text. The author recalls a railbus journey from Drogheda to Navan when the bus was stopped between Duleek and Beauparc (the station in this photo) in order to allow a hen partridge and her brood to cross the line.

JD Fitzgerald

and for a while a small buffet car operated in a return Sunday train between Derry and Bundoran. Also from about 1944 onwards the 'Bundoran Express' included a restaurant or buffet car in its make-up, but these vehicles did not operate west of Clones. The up and down 'Bundoran Expresses' crossed at Pettigo, while the catering vehicle ran between Dublin and Clones only. Working the 'Bundoran Expresses' on the Irish North part of their journey was now a job for Dundalk shed (Dundalk–Pettigo and return), whilst before the war Clones shed organised the Clones–Bundoran–Omagh–Clones run. Each of these jobs in its day provided some mileage money to supplement the basic wages of the drivers and firemen concerned. Total mileages were 170 for the Dundalk set and 167½ for the Clones men.

Although I never travelled through from Belfast to Derry via Clones, it did so happen that I was in Derry on the day of the first washout, and so had the rather less than pleasurable experience of journeying in a crowded 'austerity' bus over the narrow and twisty road from Pomeroy to Dungannon. Older Northern Ireland readers may remember the 'austerity' buses – 32-seaters on Bedford chassis, with slatted wooden seats like those of the GNR(I) workmen's coaches.

Mention of buses reminds me that during the war a number of vehicles from south of the border, as well as from Britain, were used by the Northern Ireland Road Transport Board. It was a source of mystery to me why, when buses bearing on their sides such inscriptions as 'West Yorkshire' could be seen on the roads of south Down, those hired from the GSR/CIÉ and the Great Northern, which were equally prominent on the same roads, had the names of their owners painted over.

No doubt some political stupidity was at the back of this, but whether it was because the powers that were in Northern Ireland did not want to be seen to be beholden to Éire, or

whether those in Éire felt that their neutrality would be compromised by a display of GSR or GNR(I) lettering, I do not know. In any case, in view of the fact that not only did Great Northern buses at that time regularly run into Newry, Keady, Enniskillen and Derry, but that GSR/CIÉ rail passenger coaches were often hired by the Northern and used on both sides of the border throughout the war, this painting out of names, whoever was responsible, was a stupid business. To quote an example of the hiring of CIÉ coaches by the GNR(I), I may mention that during the July holidays of 1945 I saw a couple of the latest steel-panelled suburban vehicles from the DSER section at Bundoran Junction.

A major event in 1947 was the exceptionally severe weather in the early part of the year, which at its height not only stopped rail services in many parts of Ireland, due to heavy snowfalls, but, since it also paralysed transport in Britain, resulted in severe coal shortages there and in Ireland. So far as CIÉ was concerned, it was a matter of reliving the worst years of wartime, whilst the GNR(I) was appreciably worse off than it had been in those years. As I have mentioned, there had been some improvement in Dublin–Belfast passenger services in 1946, but the lack of coal reversed the situation to what it had lately been; just the three through trains each way per day.

During the worst of the shortage it was not unknown for the locomotive of the down evening express to be detached from its train at Dundalk in order to bank a goods to Adavoyle. Part of the waiting time would of course be taken up with the outgoing customs examination, during which period, and sometimes for longer, there would be no steam heat, the train becoming colder and colder and the passengers more and more morose.

As a result of the coal shortage, passenger services on the Carrickmacross and Cootehill branches were withdrawn, never to be restored, and the same fate was meted out to the Kingscourt branch (among others) of Coras Iompair Éireann.

With regard to Kingscourt, I have a memory from the summer of 1946. Travelling frequently from Dublin in the evening down Great Northern express, I would observe the train for Kingscourt, scheduled to leave the present Connolly Platform 5 (at that time Platform 1 of Amiens Street Junction, CIÉ) at the same time as the Belfast train left the GNR(I) station. The contrast between the big 'Compound' 4-4-0, with its ten or eleven bogies, and the little Atock 2-4-0, at the head of the three or four six-wheelers, was striking and has remaincd with me for over half a century.

Yet another memory of a small CIÉ engine, this time from the summer of 1947, by which time fairly reasonable supplies of coal were again available, relates to a journey from Rosslare to Dublin by the up morning connection from the Fishguard boat. I had been in England, travelling each way by the Rosslare service, recently restored after wartime interruptions and cancellations, and incidentally making my first journey over the South Eastern south of Rathnew since 1930. I cannot remember anything of particular note on the down journey, but coming home my trip was enlivened by a most spirited performance by a rebuilt J15 0-6-0 which brought the six-bogie train unaided over the entire journey, including the steep climb over the reverse curves between Avoca and Rathdrum.

A number of J15s were temporarily converted to oil-burning during 1947, as were certain other CIÉ types. I have no recollection of ever travelling behind a CIÉ oil burner, but I have one memory of such a journey on the GNR(I). The latter company converted six engines to use oil fuel, and it was planned to adapt several more, with the equipment actually ordered, only to be cancelled when the coal situation improved in the early summer of 1947. The engines converted were T2 class 4-4-2Ts Nos 1, 2, 115 and 116, LQG class 0-6-0 No 159, and S class 4-4-0 No 172, *Slieve Donard*. The tank engines worked on the Dublin suburban services, and so far as I recollect, though I am not positive about this, No 159 operated over the southern end of the system. No 172, however, got further afield. When I had my journey behind her as an oil-burner she was working the 17.40 Belfast–Warrenpoint train. Unfortunately, all did not go as well as it should have. We were very late into Warrenpoint and during the journey the loco emitted wreaths of black smoke – the passengers on that particular train were not impressed by the possibilities of oil firing.

But aside from the 'big freeze', 'Compounds' as bankers, J15s as mainline express locos, and oil firing, the main event of 1947 was the inauguration of the 'Enterprise' non-stop passenger service between Belfast and Dublin. However, as I was living in south Down, all my frequent journeys to each mainline terminus started at Warrenpoint, and so it was some time before I made my own first 'Enterprise' trip. For the time being, so far as novelty on the Great Northern was concerned, I had to content myself with travelling in the refurbished restaurant car No 457, a veteran dating from 1905. Though still retaining its clerestory roof, centre kitchen, coal-fired cooker and tip-up seats (for a total of no less then 42 persons), it had been rebuilt after suffering damage by fire in the Dundalk paint shop, and had emerged from the works with wide windows with sliding top lights and a redecorated interior. For some time after its reappearance this old car ran in the 08.15 up express, returning to Belfast in the early afternoon train. A short time after I had the opportunity of observing the novelty of this facelifted old vehicle, I was provided with another innovation of considerably greater interest – the sight of 'Compound' No 87 *Kestrel* arriving in Goraghwood at the head of the 08.15, equipped with a Belpaire firebox, the first of those which ultimately became standard on all five of the V class locos.

An interesting preliminary to the introduction of the 'Enterprise' was the restoration of the manning of engines working through between Belfast and Dublin and return by a single set of men. Up until the time of the 1932 strike, four out of the five daily through engine workings each way on weekdays had been operated by three Dublin sets and one Belfast set, leaving one return service to be shared between Dundalk and Belfast sheds, with crews changing over at the former town. After the strike through working on weekdays ceased, all crews changing at Dundalk, though some through working on Sundays remained. The restoration of city to city working by one crew in late 1945 was partial and concerned the 12.00 up train and the balancing down evening service. It was while working the 12.00 with S2 class No 190, *Lugnaquilla*, that Adelaide driver Billy Bryan was killed when a connecting rod big end failed coming down Rush bank, about 15 miles north of Dublin, the rod going through the firebox. Inspector Green of Dublin who was travelling on the engine was also killed, whilst fireman Sam Snowden of Adelaide was invalided off duty for a long time and thereafter never resumed footplate work.

8 Introduction to the NCC

I have mentioned that from 1944 onwards I came increasingly into contact with the NCC. Here are a few recollections of that company.

The first memory concerns a short trip which probably few Irish railway enthusiasts, and proportionately fewer still members of the general public now living, have ever made; this was over the entire length of the narrow gauge line from Derry (Victoria Road) to Strabane. I know that at the time this line was the property of the London Midland and Scottish Railway, and not of its Irish subsidiary the NCC, but for practical purposes this short section, though worked by the County Donegal Railways Joint Committee (itself jointly owned by the GNR(I) and the LMS) was an NCC line. The occasion of the journey, which I think took place in 1947, when I was still working as a trainee valuer, was as follows.

For some reason which I never discovered, but which probably had to do with taxation allowances, the NCC Accountant's department wanted to know what had been the cost of building the stations on the aforesaid line. Since most of the company's records had been destroyed during one of the air raids on Belfast in 1941, no figures were available. This seems strange since the line had been built before World War One by the then Midland Railway, and so the relevant papers might have been expected to be in the LMS archives. However, they seem to have been transferred to Belfast at some time before 1939. In any event, armed with a few figures for pre-1914 construction costs of such items as single-story brick and corrugated iron buildings and various types of platform, I set off from Derry in a bogie carriage of the County Donegal Railways Joint Committee, hauled by one of the large superheated 2-6-4Ts of that highly individual

railway. At each stop – Newbuildings, Desertone, Cullion, Donemana and the rest – I stuck my head out of the window, took a hasty glance at the station and its buildings (and repeated the process at the other side if the stop was at a crossing loop), made a rough estimate of dimensions, and recorded these and the nature of the relevant construction in my notebook. Next day at my desk I applied construction figures to dimensions and the job was done – after all, with records lost and presumably none of the original engineers or contractors alive, who could query my findings?

The engine and train were from the Donegal Company, as they always had been. Neither Midland nor LMS ever worked this outpost of their systems, though, after the demise of the Ballymoney to Ballycastle narrow gauge section of the NCC, some corridor coaches, built for the boat trains on the narrow gauge Ballymena–Larne line, became redundant and were transferred to the Donegal Railways and hence came sometimes to run on ex-LMS metals.

So far as I could see, and I was a fairly frequent visitor to Strabane in the 1950s, the main reason for keeping open the CDR Derry–Strabane narrow gauge line after the war was to enable the CDR locos to get to Derry for coaling. In the 1950s the CDR Derry–Strabane workings were the only regularly scheduled passenger trains to be operated by CDR steam engines, all other timetabled services being by railcars.

I have heard it said that during the war the CDR Derry–Strabane line was looked on with some favour by the British authorities since, not crossing the border as the GNR(I) did between Strabane and Derry, it formed a link in an alternative Belfast–Derry rail route to that of the NCC which was wholly within Northern Ireland. This facilitated troop movements from Londonderry port to Tyrone and Fermanagh, particularly that of incoming Americans.

Taking into account the very severe restrictions on road transport during the war, it is an interesting exercise of the imagination to try and picture what the tranship operations at Strabane would have been like had the main NCC Derry route been out of action for any length of time. This latter possibility, however, was always fairly remote in view of the existence of a Great Northern as well as an NCC line between Belfast and Antrim, and the availability of the Derry central line between Cookstown Junction and Macfin.

A final memory of Strabane was of how the station staff there bore on their caps the intriguing initials 'LMS & GN'. This was because there was one station master for two stations – the GNR(I) and the CDR. All staff, apart from locomotive staff, served both stations and were paid jointly by both companies. (Presumably before the Grouping of the British railways in 1923 the legend on the caps had been 'M&GN', or was it 'MR and GN' in order to avoid confusion with the Midland and Great Northern (England) Joint Line in the east of England?).

My next memories concern Cookstown in County Tyrone, a town which, as well as claiming to have the longest main street in Ireland, was served by both the Great Northern and the Northern Counties railways. I have often wondered just how large a goods traffic the place generated in days gone by. In addition to the two separate but adjoining passenger stations, two engine sheds and the normal sized Great Northern goods yard, there was a very considerable amount of goods accommodation on the NCC side, including a large store in an area known as the market yard, to the west of the main goods installations.

It is likely that, as elsewhere on the NCC, linen and agricultural products were the staple outward items, and coal (for the linen mills) the main provider of inwards revenue. In connection with traffic in farm produce, I remember hearing at York Road that there was a direct correlation between the prosperity (or lack of it) of the south Wales coal mines and goods receipts on the NCC. The reason given for what, at first sight, seems a somewhat unlikely state of affairs was that when the miners in south Wales were earning relatively good money the demand for fish and chips increased, and hence also the demand for potatoes from Northern Ireland. No doubt as soon as the war was over and passenger traffic, particularly away from the main and Larne lines, began to decrease, the NCC cherished all the potato revenue it could get.

I remember an occasion during the winter of 1945–46 when my father and I travelled by car with some senior officers of the NCC from Belfast to Cookstown, in connection with a compensation claim against the British government in respect of railway accommodation (the market yard store) taken over and used by troops during the war. Immediately to the west of the River Bann crossing at Toomebridge, where the railway and the road used to run side by side, a passenger train from either the Derry central line or the Cookstown branch was seen approaching. As the train passed, one of the NCC men said, "All the passengers are looking out of the windows." The response from one of his colleagues was, "Is he?" There were few illusions in high places about the extent of passenger traffic west of Cookstown Junction even several years before the closure of the lines concerned.

I have just mentioned a claim for compensation against the British government as a result of military occupation of railway

LMS(NCC) U2 class 4-4-0 No 84, Lisanoure Castle, *at Portrush in 1933. Despite the relative modernity of this almost perfect example of a Midland (England) locomotive, the traversing jack at the side of the smokebox and the 'breadcart' tender are relics of a former age. Note the snatcher, for tablet working on single lines, on the side of the cab.* W Robb

premises; here is a story of another claim involving the Northern Counties Committee and his Britannic Majesty's War Department, but one in which a prominent boys' school was also involved. Early in World War Two, the governors of the elite Belfast boarding school Campbell College were informed that the War Department was about to take over their school for use as a military hospital. At about the same time the directors of the NCC were given reason to fear that their Northern Counties Hotel at Portrush was on the list for acquisition for the use of the brutal and licentious soldiery. Not for nothing did Northern Ireland have a reputation as a place where everyone in the establishment knew everyone else, and where the 'old boy' network flourished. The said network immediately went into operation with the result that whilst indeed staff and students of Campbell College had to vacate their buildings and retire 'for the duration' to Portrush, the Northern Counties

directors counted themselves lucky to have acquired as tenants of their hotel the nicely mannered and well disciplined scions of the Northern Ireland upper crust, rather than the brutal and licentious types aforementioned. Was there ever a greater illusion than that under which the innocent railway directors laboured from 1940 until the winter of 1944–45?

During the last few months of the war in Europe, as more and more British and American troops left Northern Ireland for operations on the continent, a start was made with handing back requisitioned buildings to their owners. Invariably, where such buildings had been used as living accommodation, fairly hefty compensation claims were involved. The brutal and licentious were no respecters of property. It must be acknowledged, however, that the military were but apprentice vandals compared to the adolescent Campbellians.

Negotiations over the handing back of the Northern Counties Hotel, Portrush, started at the end of 1944, as the army had given up Campbell College earlier that year. My father was the railway company's assessor and, acting with him, I was involved in the inspection of, and compiling the report on, the premises. It would be straying too far from the railway theme of these reminiscences to go into any detail regarding the state in which we found the interior of the building, but when I mention that the boys slept two or three to each small bedroom, rather than in conventional dormitories, it will be realised that supervision after they had ostensibly retired to bed was virtually impossible. Holes were kicked in plasterboard panels, taps were pulled or otherwise removed from basins, sundry illegal and dangerous electrical connections were made to sockets, and ways were found, entailing physical damage, of getting into the normally locked-up indoor swimming pool. They must have had a glorious time!

However, we must return to the railway. Before becoming shunted onto the siding at Portrush, I was recalling Cookstown. Some years after the war a Portadown driver told me a story of his cleaning days at the latter station. Before the 1932 strike, both NCC and GNR(I) each had an engine shedded overnight at Cookstown, the sheds sited not many yards apart and in each of them a solitary cleaner comprised the entire night staff. One night the Great Northern cleaner, feeling lonely (the actual word my informant used), took a walk across to the NCC shed to have a little chat with his opposite number. When he arrived he found his colleague on the footplate of the engine he was supposed to be cleaning, lying down fast asleep with his feet in the air supported by the firehole door chain.

The above example of informal liaison between Great Northern and Northern Counties reminds me that, due to the effect of the war on traffic and the greatly increased government involvement in all aspects of transport in Northern Ireland, the war years saw a high degree of official cooperation between the GNR(I) and the NCC, and between each of these companies and the BCDR.

Cooperation extended south of the border, in that engineering work was carried out at Dundalk for both NCC and BCDR. An example of operational cooperation was the running of military special trains over lines of more than one of the three companies, such trains often having to be provided at short notice and over unusual routes. One operation, related to me after the war, involved the running of a train from Belfast to Newcastle over the BCDR, after which it reversed and travelled to Castlewellan and thence over the Great Northern to Scarva on the Great Northern main line. Here another reversal took place to enable the train to get to Portadown, only to undergo a third change of direction before proceeding via the Derry Road to its ultimate destination, Omagh. It would be interesting to know what was the engine power over the approximately 72 miles from Belfast (Queen's Quay) to Portadown, particularly in view of the weight restrictions over the BCDR lines and those of the Northern between Castlewellan and Scarva.

A fairly regular military special which ran during the war was a 'leave train' from Larne to Omagh (and thence to Strabane and also Enniskillen) via the Greenisland Viaduct, Antrim, Lisburn and Portadown. Catering facilities were provided on this train in the shape of one of the old Great Northern centre-kitchen dining cars.

While on the subject of troop specials to Enniskillen, it can be noted that, despite Irish Free State neutrality, the section of the Great Northern from the border between Tynan and Glaslough to the other part of that imaginary line just west of Clones was frequently in use when these trains ran. Often, when a large

Belfast and County Down large 0-6-0 No 10 at Comber. Although this locomotive and sister engine No 4 were primarily goods engines, they occasionally appeared on passenger trains.   W Robb

The long-lived (1892–1951) 0-6-0 No 26 of the Belfast and County Down Railway on a down train at Knock, in the eastern suburbs of Belfast. This small machine, which saw much service on the Donaghadee branch, was, above all other engines, the company's maid of all work. Although this photo dates from the1930s, it could have been taken at any time up to the closure of the main line. The (in)famous Co Down six-wheelers lasted until the end.   W Robb

number of military personnel had to be transported to Enniskillen or other parts of County Fermanagh, several trains would be required. The first train would proceed to Omagh (though not usually by the roundabout route just described) where a fresh engine would be waiting to take it forward towards Enniskillen. As soon as the train had departed for Fermanagh, the engine which had brought it to Omagh from Portadown or Belfast would be turned and so be ready to take the second train onwards to its destination. The process would be repeated until the last train had departed for Enniskillen, leaving one loco at Omagh, which had been the position before the arrival of train number one.

In order to avoid congesting the single line between Enniskillen and Omagh by the returning empty carriage trains, the latter would travel back to the Portadown/Belfast area via Clones, Monaghan and Armagh. No doubt some balancing of staffs was required after such an operation, but this would have been a small price to pay for avoiding the headaches of numerous single line crossings, and also congestion at Enniskillen station, shed and turntable.

The peripheral involvement of officially neutral Irish Free State territory in facilitating troop movements in Northern Ireland was paralleled by the use, as circumstance required, of engines shedded in Dublin and elsewhere in Éire to help with heavy special train movements in Northern Ireland. As I wrote in an article in an *IRRS Journal* some years ago, I remember being at Amiens Street shed one afternoon in 1943 when the total stock of engines on view was two: a 'Compound' which had brought in the 12 noon passenger from Belfast, and a solitary 4-4-2T. All other machines had gone north to assist in some major troop movement. No doubt they returned with rather more coal in their tenders than there had been on departure.

However, empty troop trains running

between Clones and the Armagh border, and Dublin, Drogheda and Dundalk engines on temporary loan to Adelaide and Portadown, were only occasional phenomena in the wartime day-to-day operation of the Great Northern. It was a different matter regarding the transfer of staff. The reduction in the number of services (though not in the overall traffic figures) south of the border, coupled with the great increase in the number of trains running in Northern Ireland, resulted in the transfer of many enginemen.

Until after the war, transfer and promotion in the loco department was on an all-line basis, with the result that there were Dundalk and Clones men working out of Portadown and Belfast, and at least one fireman who had started his railway career in Oldcastle was now based in Derry. The demand for footplate staff also meant that any former enginemen still unemployed as a result of the 1932 strike, and who were prepared to resume railway work, were speedily re-engaged.

A visible indication of the widespread transferring of drivers and firemen was that one could scarcely ever travel in a mainline cross-border train which was not carrying several enginemen as passengers. For example, a man from Dundalk temporarily attached to Portadown or Adelaide sheds might well continue to live at home and save the lodging allowance, while his Dublin or Drogheda colleagues could easily do the same if stationed in Portadown or Newry. Another sign of the times as regards footplate men was the reduction in the average age of firemen: young men recently employed in cleaning could now be regularly seen firing to experienced drivers old enough to be their fathers, and elderly fathers at that.

It was commonly said that firing to one's father was not a practice which was encouraged by the Great Northern. Two explanations were offered for this. The first explanation was that in the event of an accident involving the deaths of a father and son, a family would suffer a double bereavement. The second reason was that if one or both members of a family team survived an accident, it might be difficult to get evidence incriminating one engineman from the other. Am I being cynical in suggesting that whilst no Mechanical Engineer or Running Superintendent would want any engineman's family to suffer a double bereavement, nevertheless the cold official view of the Company, as distinct from the personal feelings of senior officers, was that the avoidance of difficulty in obtaining evidence after the accident was the primary reason for the ban on what we may describe as 'family footplates'.

I have mentioned that staff other than enginemen were transferred from Éire to Northern Ireland as a result of the war. Many such moves, as was the case with loco crews, were temporary, and the people concerned returned to their original areas in due course. There were, however, two interesting moves of administrative departments which remained permanent. These were the transfer of the headquarters of the Eastern District Engineer from Dundalk to Belfast, and the migration of the Hotels and Catering Manager between the same two locations.

We have just been considering possible accidents – now a few words regarding two actual ones, each of which may be considered as being primarily due to wartime conditions. These occurred at Straboe, on the main line of the GSW section of CIÉ, and at Ballymacarret, close to the junction of the main line and the Bangor branch of the BCDR. Since each of these two tragic happenings have been fully described in Journals of the Irish Railway Record Society – Straboe by David Murray and Ballymacarret by Desmond Coakham – there is no need for me to go into the details of either. I mention them merely to record a couple of personal reminiscences.

I first heard of the Straboe crash on the second morning after it happened, in the booking office at Warrenpoint station, and I mention this to indicate the free and relaxed atmosphere at GNR(I) country stations. It was a cold, raw and foggy morning, and I was on my way to Dublin by the early morning service, the 08.40 from Warrenpoint, connecting at Goraghwood with the 08.15 from Belfast. There was a good fire in the booking-cum-parcel office, where a few passengers had foregathered for a warm-up before boarding the train. Also present, in addition to the booking clerk, were the enginemen and guard of the 08.40. The topic of conversation was the possible cause of the Straboe collision.

My second recollection is that it was the restriction on the use of 'push-pulls' on the BCDR, after the Ballymacarret accident, that led to the introduction of a Great Northern triplet articulated railcar to operate inner suburban services between Belfast and Holywood.

9 New Locomotives, 1947–1950

As well as the inauguration of the non-stop 'Enterprise' service on the GNR(I), the year 1947 saw the delivery of ten new steam locomotives to that company by Beyer Peacock. These engines, Nos 201–05 (4-4-0s) and Nos 145–49 (0-6-0s), were of Classes U and UG respectively and were generally similar to U class Nos 196–200 of 1915 and UG class Nos 78–82 of 1937. All 20 machines were tender versions of the standard T2 class 4-4-2Ts.

Superficial differences between the 1947 locomotives and their predecessors were that the boilers were pitched rather higher on account of improvements to the crank webs and bearings, and that the rather ugly pattern of side-window cab, which had been introduced on Nos 78–82, was provided for the new 4-4-0s, as well as being continued on the UGs. Nos 201–05 were painted blue and named *Meath*, *Louth*, *Armagh*, *Antrim* and *Down* respectively, a move which led to the subsequent bestowing of blue paint and names (Loughs) on the five original 4-4-0s of Class U. I have always thought it a pity that the Q class were never similarly treated. I was interested to hear from the late Harry Wilson, the last Great Northern Mechanical Engineer, when I was speaking to him one day soon after the break-up of the Great Northern, that he felt this should have been done.

To return to the new locos: as compared to

No 149, one of the 1947 batch of GNR(I) Class UG 0-6-0s, on what was probably a substitute for a railcar or railbus working at Duleek, on the Oldcastle branch.

A Donaldson, courtesy WT Scott

the traditional 2,500 gallon tenders with flared sides of Nos 196–200 and the high-sided 3,500 gallon ones supplied to the 1937 0-6-0s, the tenders of all ten new engines were high-sided, but of only 2,500 gallons capacity, and to a pattern closely resembling the LMS Stanier design. Differences which were not immediately apparent, in addition to the crank changes, were an improved type of tyre fastening and 200 lb per square inch boiler pressure, which latter feature had appeared on the 1947 UGs. However, in their last years all 15 of the 200 lb engines worked at 175 lb, as the five original Us did all their lives.

Building of new mainline carriages to existing designs continued at Dundalk in 1947 and 1948 and included the conversion of workmen's coaches to standard K15 thirds. An innovation in carriage building was the production of full first and brake first side-corridor stock. These vehicles were intended primarily for the 'Enterprise' services, which in 1948 were doubled to comprise a Dublin-based as well as Belfast-based operation.

The times of these services were down (ex-Dublin) at 11.00 and 17.30, and up (ex-Belfast) at 10.30 and 16.45. The morning up and evening down trains, always the more heavily loaded, were normally 'Compound' hauled (at least until the arrival of the new large 4-4-0s shortly to be referred to). The balancing Dublin set – except for the inaugural run, when 'Compound' No 83 Eagle was used – was normally headed by an S class 4-4-0.

The overall schedule for all four trains either way was two hours and 15 minutes, leaden footed to what would have been the case in 1932 and 12 to 15 minutes longer than what would have been the probable allowance had the trains been introduced at anytime during the period 1933–39.

However, the quality of coal available and the arrears of maintenance of permanent way and locomotives applying in those early post-war years meant that the schedules were as keen as could be expected. This was especially so in the case of the 10.30–17.30 trains, which in the earlier years of their running were sometimes loaded to nine bogies and were operated by the 'Compounds' whose tenders were of only 3,500 gallons capacity.

I have already mentioned that I did not make my first 'Enterprise' journey until sometime after the commencement of the service. It was in the early spring of 1950, just outside the chronological limit which I have set for these reminiscences, that I first travelled on one of these new trains. The six-bogie formation was working the 11.00 ex-Amiens Street, the locomotive being S class No 171 Slieve Gullion. There was nothing outstanding in the running, although time was kept despite a momentary stop in Dundalk, and of course the overall 70 mph speed limit.

The Dundalk stop, to pick up Northern Ireland customs officers who conducted their examinations on the train during its onward journey to Belfast, was a regular feature of the schedule at the time, but the arrangement was short-lived. My main recollection of this journey relates neither to locomotive nor customs men, but rather to the internal transformation which had been carried out on buffet car No 266, with seating reduced from 40 to 30 and the provision of prints of Humbert Craig paintings of Irish scenery, among other items. Had I known at the time that some 17 years later I was to be involved in the preservation of No 171 (happily still with us and in regular operation under the auspices of the Railway Preservation Society of Ireland), I would no doubt have paid more attention to the engine and less to the catering vehicle. As it was, I was merely regretful that our 'horse' was Slieve Gullion – I had hoped that we might have had No 173 Galteemore, generally reckoned to be the best of the S class.

I have referred to the 3,500 gallon tenders of the 'Compounds' and have implied that this relatively small capacity was one of the

Different types of motive power for the Cork–Dublin–Belfast 'Enterprise' express during the early 1950s. The upper picture is of ex-GSWR/GSR 400 class 4-6-0 No 405 of Coras Iompair Éireann about to leave Cork. In the lower illustration we have Great Northern Railway (Ireland) 3-cylinder compound No 87, Kestrel, about to take the train on from Dublin to Belfast. Alongside No 405 is 'Woolwich' 2-6-0 No 390, whilst the Northern engine has as its companion sister loco No 86, Peregrine, *waiting in one of the carriage storage roads before heading the 18.30 train to Belfast.* S Kennedy

GNR(I) Class VS 3-cylinder 4-4-0 No 209, Foyle, *before the fitting of smoke deflectors and front number plate. Note the absence of any coupling on the front drawhook. Subsequently a three link chain, standard for all Great Northern engines, other than the 4-4-2Ts and 2-4-2Ts, the UG 0-6-0s and the 1947 batch of U class 4-4-0s, was provided.*
GNR(I) official photograph, courtesy S Kennedy

deterrents to any shorter time than 2¼ hours being scheduled for the 'Enterprise' journey. During 1948, however, this particular drawback became less relevant, although the schedules remained unaltered. The reason was the delivery, again by Beyer Peacock, of five new large 4-4-0s of Class VS which were a three-cylinder 'simple' development of the 'Compounds'.

There is no need for me to go into any detail about these fine machines, the last 4-4-0s to be built in Europe, since numerous descriptions and photographs of them have appeared over the past 50 years. Perhaps I may be permitted, however, to record one or two personal impressions from the time when they appeared.

For some time before the arrival of the VS locos it had been fairly common knowledge that they were on the way, but so far as I at any rate was concerned, no precise details were available. I must confess that when I saw the first press photograph I was slightly

disappointed, the outward resemblance to the 'Compounds' being so close. I, and no doubt other interested but non-technical people, had been hoping for something radically different; even perhaps a 'Mogul'. I was surprised that in 1948 side-window cabs had not been provided, and to my mind the almost slavish copying of an LMS design of tender was unenterprising (no pun intended). Another apparent LMS feature, although no doubt it was entirely fortuitous, was that on a front, or three quarter front, view after the fitting of smoke deflectors these engines had a more than superficial resemblance to the original 'Baby Scots'. As 4-4-0s and not 4-6-0s maybe they could have been described as premature 'Baby Scots'.

However, 'handsome is as handsome does' is as relevant a maxim for railway locomotives as it is for anything else, and the VS engines soon settled down to regular duties on the Belfast-based 'Enterprise' and other mainline turns. In their early days Nos 206, 207 and

208, *Liffey*, *Boyne* and *Lagan* respectively, were based at Adelaide, whilst Amiens Street shed had No 209 *Foyle* and No 210 *Erne*. Despite what I have said about the Dublin-based 'Enterprise' being usually headed by a S class loco, I remember seeing No 210 working that train once or twice.

It was a great pity that the situation as regards coal and track maintenance at the time the VS class was introduced, closely followed by the diesel revolution, resulted in the new engines never having the chance to realise their full potential. It was, however, established by the authorities in Dundalk that, operating on similar duties to those of the 'Compounds', the VSs were rather lighter on coal than were the earlier engines. This finding was most interesting in view of the fact that both classes had identical boilers and fireboxes. One possible explanation for the failure of the 'Compounds' to show the economy in coal consumption, of which they should theoretically have been capable, was that they were operating at boiler pressures below those for which they were designed, thus upsetting the optimum relationship between high and low pressure cylinders. This, however, is conjecture on my part. I do know that it was often found at times of heavy repairs to the 'Compounds' that there was greater wear on the big end bearings of the high-pressure cylinders than that of the low pressures, thus indicating that for an individual engine the inside hp cylinder was doing a disproportionate amount of work.

I have always regretted that the time when I was travelling frequently on steam locomotives coincided with the declining years of the 'Compounds' and of the VS class. I had several runs on these big 4-4-0s, one of which

To see a piloted VS 4-4-0 entering Amiens Street station, Dublin, was rare indeed. The VS in this picture is unidentifiable, but is not 206 or 209, which had higher smoke deflectors. The pilot engine is rebuilt S class 4-4-0 No 173 Galteemore. In the summer of 1938 she was timed, at least twice, at just over 90 mph on the up Mail between Adavoyle and Dundalk. The building whose roof is just visible over the top of the train is Amiens Street shed, whilst the open wagon is on one of the approach roads to Sherriff Street goods yard.

Kelland Collection, courtesy JD Fitzgerald

I described at great length in 'Steam Finale'; nevertheless, how pleasant it would have been to have been able to include among my Great Northern recollections a trip on a V or a VS taking ten bogies over the Wellington bank on a 25-minute schedule. Whether on an up journey any notes written when coming down the bank through Mount Pleasant would have been legible is open to doubt.

Although the 15 U, UG and VS engines of 1947 and 1948 were the last new steam locomotives obtained by the Great Northern, they were not the only new machines to appear on Irish railways after World War Two. The first ten 2-6-4Ts (the 'Jeeps') for the NCC came out in 1946 and 1947, followed by eight more in 1949 and 1950. However, my experience of them dates only from 1950, whilst it was 1953 before I saw *Lough Erne* or *Lough Melvin,* the last 0-6-4Ts to come to the Sligo, Leitrim and Northern Counties Railway. It is good to remember, however, that I did get around to footplating on one of these interesting little machines (it was my good fortune to travel many hundreds of miles on 'Jeeps'), even if only on the prosaic duties of shunting at Queen's Quay, Belfast, and subsequently heading a freight train thence over the central railway to Grosvenor Street Goods Yard.

One final recollection from 1948 and 1949 remains to be chronicled. In the former year my father was asked by GNR(I) management to carry out a valuation, for insurance purposes, of all buildings on the system. This was not a particularly arduous task as far as making the valuation was concerned, but it was one which took a fair amount of time and entailed a considerable amount of travelling. As the junior end of the partnership, it was appropriate that I should do the lion's share of the getting around; needless to say that with my great interest in railways, and the Great Northern in particular, I had no objection to this. And so, starting in the summer of 1948, I realised what might be described as an Irish railway enthusiast's dream: a first class 'all stations' pass and mandate to visit every station and building on the GNR(I).

Most of my travelling in connection with the insurance job was done by rail, though not always. For instance, where passenger services had been withdrawn, or the timetable precluded a 'there and back' journey from Warrenpoint plus an inspection or inspections on the same day, a railway staff car had to be used. Examples of one-day car journeys were from Dundalk to Inniskeen, Essexford, Carrickmacross, Keady and Markethill; from Belfast to several Antrim branch stations; and from Omagh (which at the time still boasted a District Superintendent and staff car) to some Bundoran branch stations.

The Bundoran branch foray included travelling by train between Ballyshannon and Bundoran, whilst car and driver went off to the GNR(I) bus garage in Donegal town in order to have some mechanical defect seen to. I well remember this trip, not so much on its own account as for the return rail journey from Omagh. Due to my colleague's unscheduled trip to Donegal, we were too late to connect with the up Derry Mail which left Omagh at 17.00, and so I had to avail of the following 'all stations' railcar as far as Dungannon.

The car was one of the articulated 'C' vehicles which, as well as providing for the common people, accommodated six first class passengers in comparative luxury in separate armchair seats at the back of the vehicle. In years to come I travelled the Derry Road many times in conventional coaches, in AEC and BUT railcars (and survived the 'storm at sea' antics of the latter over the bog between Annaghmore and Vernersbridge), and on the footplates of GNR(I) engines and NCC 'Moguls', which latter rivalled the BUTs for liveliness.

However, the most distinctive and memorable of all these journeys was on this occasion, as the sole first class passenger, sitting in state in my armchair at the rear of the railcar as it clanked its way with ringing coupling rods at its full 40 mph, stopping at Beragh, Sixmilecross, Carrickmore, Pomeroy and Donaghmore, rounding reverse curves, climbing up and running down banks, in and out of holes and over level crossings, all in the process of providing a closer, more intimate view of the surrounding countryside than would have been available from my first class seat in the prestigious and somewhat faster Derry Mail.

But now, seated (in memory, if not reality) in my luxurious armchair, watching the invariable swarm of rabbits feeding and playing in the field to the south of the line at the foot of Carrickmore bank, it is time for me to close these random recollections.

Tomorrow I am scheduled to travel from my present home near Sydney to Gosford on the 'central coast' of New South Wales in an air-conditioned and comfortable double-decked EMU train, through some of the most spectacular wood and water scenery of eastern Australia. I will enjoy every minute of the trip and will be keenly interested in all that I may see on the railway. Nevertheless, I would gladly swap this journey for the sight of a 'Woolwich' on the up Mail at Mullingar, or a winter night's run from Goraghwood to Warrenpoint with 'the Bacon' Quinn on No 74, demonstrating his contempt for extended schedules.

Bibliography

Clements, RN and Robbins, JM, *ABC of Irish Locomotives*, Ian Allan, 1949

Donaldson, D, McDonnell, B and O'Neill, Jack, *A Decade of Steam on CIÉ*, Railway Preservation Society of Ireland, nd

Hamilton Ellis, C, *The North British Railway*, Ian Allan, 1959

Johnston, Norman, *Locomotives of the GNR(I)*, Colourpoint Books, 1999

Journal of the Irish Railway Record Society, various dates

Knock, OS, *L.N.E.R. Steam*, David and Charles, 1969

Vallance, HA, *The Highland Railway*, David and Charles, 1969

General Index

Italics indicate an illustration of or relating to the subject.

Index of Locomotive Classes
Italics indicate an illustration of or relating to the subject.